Praise for Hans Gerhardt's HotelBiz

"Against all odds Hans Gerhardt's remarkable story goes from growing up in war-torn poverty of Germany to hosting kings and queens
in Canada—and along the way overcoming tragedy and turning it into
triumph time and again. *HotelBiz* is an extraordinarily intimate story
of how he became 'the hotelier to the stars' and the adventures that
arose from being the 'host with the most' as the world's best hotelier.
The book is a very personal journey of overcoming grief and finding success. Its everything you ever wanted to know about what goes
on at one of the world's swankiest star-studded 'homes of hospitality'—and you'll even find a couple of secrets about me I'd forgotten!
HotelBiz is the VIP key to unlock the door for a very suite inside look
at the lifestyles of the rich and famous."

   Robin Leach, television personality

"A riveting and often most touching life story. It brings back great
nostalgia for the good ol' Sutton Place days when Hans was stylishly
at the helm."

   Christopher Plummer, actor

"A must read for hoteliers and their staffers and guests the world over,
this is an engrossing odyssey of daring, youthful adventure…his rec-
ollections are handsomely served in this autobiography."

   George Christy, the *Beverly Hills Courier*

"From von Braun to the shocking tragedy of 9/11, a story of courage
and perseverance. Simply grabs your attention."

   Eric Braeden, star of *The Young and the Restless*

"Having shot two TV series and three movies in Toronto, and having made the Sutton Place Hotel my home away from home, I can say with some authority that Hans Gerhardt's memoir is charming, insightful, amusing and captures the spirit and essence of the hotel biz he knows better than anyone else."

Michael Sloan, writer/executive producer

"It is a most worthwhile read."

Paul Godfrey, president, *National Post*

"An insightful, amusing, funny, tragic and triumphant story of a young man who makes a new life in a new land. A skilled hotelier who actually cared for his staff as much as his guests, Hans sailed through life marrying his sweetheart Helga, raising a family, and excelling in his craft promoting Toronto. September 11 changed everything. Hans lost a son and a future daughter-in-law in that horrific world trade center attack. As I comforted them in those difficult days, I marveled that despite their loss and pain, they cared so much about our city and it's people. Hans and Helga turned a tragedy into a legacy of hope and friendship between New York City and Toronto that will endure."

Randy A. Daniels, Former Secretary of State, State of New York

"*HotelBiz* is very interesting, reflecting Han's true passion for life. What is so beautiful about it is how it reflects his humanity in relating his exceptional rapport with all the characters he met throughout his career. A relevant book on human relationships."

Antoine Corinthios, president Four Seasons Hotels & Resorts, Europe, Middle East and Africa

A Memoir

To
3ANDY!

BEST WISHES

Hotel Biz

A Memoir

Hans J. Gerhardt

West-End
Books

Library and Archives Canada Cataloguing in Publication

Gerhardt, Hans J., 1941 –
     HotelBiz: a memoir / Hans J. Gerhardt.

ISBN 978–0–9736955-2-6

1.Gerhardt, Hans J., 1941 -. 2. Hotelkeepers—Ontario—Toronto—Biography.
3. Hospitality industry. I. Title

TX910.5.GA7A3 2010   647.94092   C2010-906741-X

West-End Books
80 Front St. East, Suite 605
Toronto, Ontario
Canada M5E 1T4

Cover Design: Grant Design Ltd.
Text Design: Ric Base
Electronic formatting: Ric Base

"Taste of Canada" is a registered trademark of Hans J. Gerhardt
www.HotelBiz.com

First Edition

In memory of Ralph Gerhardt.

June 6 1967 - September 11 2001.

To the world he was one of the victims of 9/11.

To us, he was the world.

Valentine's Day 1998, Statue of Liberty, New York.

Prologue

At 8:48 on a beautiful September 11 morning in 2001, Helga and I were finishing breakfast when we got the phone call that would change our lives forever.

Already it had been a tough year for us. I had been treated for prostate cancer, and Helga was diagnosed with melanoma. What's more, after a lifetime in the hotel business, I had just lost my job.

The phone call was from our son Ralph. He worked as vice president of Derivative Bonds at Cantor Fitzgerald on the 105th floor in Tower One of the World Trade Center.

Six feet, two inches tall, blue-eyed and relatively fearless at the age of 34, Ralph was always quick to the point, particularly when it came to telephone conversations. This morning, there was a quiver in his voice.

"Dad, something just happened here. We either got hit by a plane or bomb. I'm okay and we are okay, but we are evacuating. I love you, and I will call you later."

Knowing time was of the essence, I wished him luck and told him that we loved him too. I hung up and turned on the television—an image of a smoldering World Trade Center and the voice of CNN's Aaron Brown trying to explain what was unfolding.

Something about a plane hitting one of the towers.

I couldn't see any sign of a plane sticking out the side of the building, just smoke bellowing out of this big hole on the north side.

The gentle west wind pushed the smoke up and around Tower One, a black cloud trail drifting over the Bronx. I stared at the TV screen trying to figure out where Ralph's office was located, somewhat relieved when I remembered him describing a view overlooking the Statue of Liberty. That would mean he faced southwest. The smoke was coming from the north side of the tower, approximately 10 floors below the 105th floor where Ralph was located.

I called Helga to come to my office and have a look. She immediately grasped the seriousness of the situation. And then, as we stood there—initially we thought it was an instant replay —a second plane slammed into the second tower, creating this incredible blaze of fire. It was like a movie. It took us a few seconds to realize what was happening before our eyes.

Then a news flash: there had been an attack on the Pentagon in Washington, D.C. Our other son, Stephan, lived in Washington with his family. He worked in tourism at the Canadian Embassy.

We stayed glued to the TV, trying to be optimistic. If anyone could make it to safety, Ralph could. I knew that his girlfriend, Linda Luzzicone, worked on the same floor, along with 250 others. They would find each other in the acre-sized space and stay together.

Repeated calls to Ralph's cell phone went unanswered. I kept thinking he would be hurrying down fire stairs headed for the exit, unable to answer. I tried to compute in my mind how long that might take.

Local CTV News anchor Ken Shaw is a friend. I dialed his direct line hoping to get more information than was on the television. I told whoever answered Ken's phone who I was and that my son Ralph was in the World Trade Center. Immediately, they asked me if I would like to talk to Lisa Laflamme, the reporter anchoring CTV's news coverage that morning. Without thinking,

I said yes. As I stood there on the phone, I saw my name and then my photograph appear on the screen. I suddenly realized what I was doing. In shock, I told Lisa I had to go and hung up. We went back to trying to reach Ralph by phone.

Then Tower Two collapsed.

It was surreal. Hard to believe what was happening on live television before our eyes. Still, we clung to hope. The next thing Tower One collapsed as well! We watched in disbelief and horror. I turned off the television but that didn't last long. We turned it on again, hoping against hope we might catch sight of Ralph among the throngs of escaping New Yorkers. We never did.

As the day progressed, our phone rang non-stop. Each time we thought it might be Ralph, calling to say he was all right. But that call never came. In the meantime, our friend Elke Steinmetz and her husband Peter had come over to console us and also bring food. We had been in touch with our son, Stephan. He was all right in Dallas where he had been hosting a seminar. He was desperately trying to get back to Washington and his girlfriend, Christine.

Increasingly frightened, Helga and I decided to go to New York. Calls offering to help came from Ralph's friends Darcy Hall, Jill and Charlie Lehoczky. When Charlie heard about our plans, he immediately offered to drive us to New York and help look for Ralph. In Toronto, Stephan's friend Patrick Cappa collected dental records and X-rays from Ralph's doctors, in case they might be needed.

We left for New York on Wednesday, September 12 at one o'clock in the afternoon, another beautiful hot day. We drove because North American airspace was closed, no flights were going in or out of the U.S. It was also uncertain what the U.S.-Canada border would be like. Could we even get across?

I phoned Ontario Premier Mike Harris's office looking for help. None was forthcoming. However, a former business associate, Randy Daniels, had become New York's Secretary of State. When I telephoned him, he immediately took my call.

"When you get to the border, if there are any problems, here is my emergency cell phone number," he said. "I will be with the governor. We'll get you across the border."

Ken Shaw put us in contact with the CTV's Niagara region freelance reporter, Harry Rosettani, a former Ontario police officer who also worked for CNN and ABC. He would help us across the border in exchange for a short interview. Harry made some phone calls to U.S. Customs and Immigration and then met us at Fort Erie. We crossed the border without incident. In fact, the officer on duty saluted us and wished us luck.

The drive was solemn. We kept telling ourselves that Ralph must be somewhere, perhaps injured and unconscious in hospital. The worst case scenario we conjured had him trapped under ruins.

We reminisced about Ralph and Linda's last visit to Toronto on Labor Day; my visit in late August to New York; his visit to Toronto in July for Helga's birthday, insisting on a party for her. We talked about how Ralph came to Toronto in April so he could be here when I had my cancer operation. So many memories, including the last time he had been at our cottage and his visit to Jill and Charlie's cottage on the same trip. His university buddy Jeff Eby dropped in while he was there. Ironically, they discussed World Trade Center security. Returning late, Ralph presented Helga with a large lantern candle. We already had lots of candles scattered throughout the house

"Ralph," I told him, "we need another candle like a hole in our head."

"Dad, this one is special," he replied. "Whenever you light it, you will think of me."

It turned out to be so poignantly true. To this day, we light that candle and think of Ralph.

We arrived in New York at about 10 p.m. Crossing the George Washington Bridge, we saw smoke from the fires at the World Trade Center. We had been able to smell those fires long before we reached New York.

I looked out to the right, straight down the Hudson River with a view of all Manhattan. I should have been able to see the World Trade Center. But there were no towers, only a grey cloud rising from where they had stood. The cloud, like a huge arm over Manhattan, stretched north as far as the eye could see.

Charlie turned on the radio for the first time since we started our journey, hoping to get some news. Instead, we heard Paul McCartney singing "Yesterday, all my troubles seemed so far away…"

We listened and silently wept as we turned onto the Henry Hudson Parkway. Robin McKenna, a friend of both Ralph and Stephan, had been in contact with us. We picked her up on the way to Ralph's apartment. She was a great help with maps, phone numbers, and anything else we needed.

Waiting for us inside the apartment was Mike Minas, Ralph's friend who had quit Cantor Fitzgerald months before. Like the rest of us, Mike was in shock. Even more so since he worked across the street from the World Trade Center at the World Financial Center. When the first plane hit, he ran over to Tower One in time to see falling bodies. He stood there, staring in horror. His eyes fell upon a piece of paper on the ground—with Cantor Fitzgerald's letterhead on it.

Then the second plane hit. Mike literally felt the earth move as the plane struck Tower Two. The vacuum created made his chest hurt. Bystanders started screaming at him to run. He'd had recent back surgery and found walking difficult. Nonetheless, he turned and dashed east, clambering over a fence to find himself on FDR Drive. A passing car slowed. He threw open the door and dived in. There were three men inside. Mike shouted at the driver to get moving. He told them what had happened, and one of the men began weeping.

Eventually, they let him out in the Chinatown area, and he ran home to his apartment on Lexington Avenue and 23rd Street. He then watched from his apartment roof as the towers collapsed.

When we told Mike we were coming to New York, he hurried

over to Ralph's apartment and tried to get in. Ironically, the night before, the two friends had sat in the apartment eating hamburgers and drinking beer. Now when he tried to get inside, the landlord wouldn't allow it.

Finally, Mike called a locksmith to open the door, claiming that he lost his keys at the World Trade Center. Once inside, he found the remnants of the hamburgers he and Ralph ate the previous night.

Thanks to Mike we were able to stay at Ralph's apartment for the next month. He had a difficult time coming to terms with what he saw and the loss of Ralph and Linda and so many other Cantor Fitzgerald friends. Afterward, he could never understand the lack of compassion for the survivors who, like himself, witnessed the horrors of that day. He refuses to go back to Ground Zero.

Ralph's apartment was across from the 69th Regiment Armory at Lexington Avenue and 26th Street. The armory had been turned into a temporary family emergency center. The street filled with family members of the missing, desperately seeking information. People began to display photographs of their loved ones. A sea of photos and flowers, stuffed animals, all kinds of personal items, filled armory walls as well as nearby trees and telephone polls. Heart-wrenching to see these prayers of hope; prayers that mostly would never be answered.

When we registered, we were asked to provide hair and tooth brushes for potential DNA identification. They also took our DNA samples. The shock of what was happening really hit us at that point. It had the effect of dampening our hopes Ralph was alive. Reality was more or less confirmed at Cantor Fitzgerald's emergency center at the Pierre Hotel. We were told that no one above the 91st floor of Tower One had been found alive.

Then a phone call.

Early Thursday morning, two days after the attack, it came from David Turberfield—everyone called him Turbo—a friend of Ralph's. Turbo had moved to Tokyo, Japan. He had read on the

Internet that Ralph had been found. He was okay. I could hardly believe it.

Dressing quickly, I ran over to the emergency center where I encountered a police officer named John Trimmer. He listened to my story and then for the next five hours searched every list on every computer, and made phone call after phone call. Nothing. No one had any information about a survivor named Ralph Gerhardt.

Apparently some sadistic idiot posted Ralph's name on the Internet, listing him as alive. A terrible, sick joke. You could not believe anyone would do such a stupid, painful thing.

Our despair deepened.

Ironically, we found Linda's name listed among survivors, but it turned out this was an aunt with the same name who had escaped Tower Two. More irony: the aunt also survived the 1993 World Trade Center bombing.

Stephan and Christine finally made it to New York Friday, and we also met with Linda's parents and family. Later, our pregnant niece Tina and her husband Joe arrived from Washington. Together we continued to wait.

And hope.

Finally, 10 days after we got to the city, we were able to visit Ground Zero. Coincidentally, we ran into Officer Trimmer at Pier 94 where they had relocated the emergency center. He was finishing his shift when he heard where we were headed. He offered to come along, and we gratefully accepted his invitation.

Together we traveled to the site along the Hudson River on board a ferry while U.S. Marine craft with mounted machine guns patrolled the waters around us, and overhead the skies buzzed with low-flying fighter jets.

The boats and yachts in the tiny harbor where we docked were covered in grey dust. The devastation at the trade center site was horrifying. Metal girders jabbed a blue sky like fork prongs. A pillar from one of the towers was a giant arrow piercing the side of the nearby American Express building 20 floors up. Trees that survived were stripped of their leaves. The smell of still-smoldering fires overwhelmed everything.

Helga and I knew that our son was somewhere in all this rubble as well as thousands of other victims. Entering the site, we passed firemen, emergency workers, and police. Whenever we encountered these brave men and women, they stopped what they were doing, took off their head gear, nodded at us, and bowed their heads. They, too, knew our pain, having lost so many of their own family members and colleagues.

We watched as they worked through the debris with small buckets looking for anything that might be part of a human being or a personal possession. When they found a human body, a signal horn sounded. Immediately, everything and everybody stopped. A stretcher arrived and whatever remains had been found were loaded onto it and then draped with an American flag. A moment of silence followed. After that, the agonizing search continued. Over the next weeks, we saw this ritual repeated many times from our lawyers' offices and the 9/11 family center at Liberty Plaza, directly across from the trade center.

We encountered so many extraordinary people during those difficult days, from the caring staff at the Department of Health where they had set up the refrigerated trailers to house and identify body parts, to the police headquarters personnel trying to identify items found in the rubble. Inspector Jack Trabitz showed us around and it was touching to see how hard his staff worked to find recipients for items uncovered at Ground Zero. Unfortunately, nothing was ever found belonging to Ralph.

Reluctantly, we began to realize the time had come to let go of the search. The realization came when I had to sign Ralph's death certificate. It came again when Helga and I stood alone in the doorway of Ralph's empty apartment remembering how much he loved it; we stood there and wept.

Our visit to Ground Zero had been like looking death in the eye through the view from hell. Peering out over this ghastly scene,

I couldn't avoid thinking about my life and how I had come to this dreadful moment.

In the months that followed those days of terrible tragedy, I would do more and more soul searching. I would consider and reconsider a long journey that has taken me from the poverty of post-war Germany to, literally, the seven seas and adventures around the world, and then on to Canada and a new life and career serving the rich and the famous at the country's most prestigious hotels.

In my life, I had met kings and queens and movie stars, married a wonderful woman, raised two amazing children, and learned a thing or two along the way about triumph and tragedy.

Was the journey worth it? Many, many times following Ralph's death, I was left wondering. I keep wondering to this day.

Chapter One

My father's name was Bernhard Gerhardt. He was German but no ordinary German. A noted rocket specialist, he became, in the early 1930s, part of Germany's top secret rocket development program. Initially, he worked as a civilian employed in Kummersdorf and Bitterfeld by I.G. Farben, a giant German chemical corporation. When the Nazis came to power in 1933, they dramatically ramped up rocket design and testing. The idea was not to reach space, but to produce long-range warheads at a time when other nations were interested primarily in conventional weapons development.

Shortly after my father joined the rocket program, it was relocated to a military testing facility at Peenemünde, on an island at the mouth of the Peene River on the easternmost part of the Baltic coast. The project leader was a young man named Wernher von Braun. Like my father and other rocket specialists working at the facility, von Braun dreamed of sending a rocket to the moon, but he needed government support to realize that dream. Peenemünde was the deal with the devil that he, along with everyone else, made. Little wonder, then, that Peenemünde is known not only as the *Die Wiege der Raumschiffahrt* or Cradle of Space Explorations, but also as Hitler's *Geheime Waffen Schmiede*—Hitler's Secret Weapon Factory.

The Smithsonian's aerospace curator, Professor Michael Neufeld, wrote in his book, *Von Braun: Dreamer of Space, Engineer of War*, "Von Braun had a Faustian shadow. A man so possessed of a vision, of an intellectual hunger, that any accommodation may be justified in its pursuit and to become the 'Columbus of Space.'"

My father, who had lost his left arm below his elbow in World War I, walked with a similar Faustian shadow, I believe. He was 15 years older than many of his colleagues, and so might have had a clearer view of what was going on, but, nonetheless, he went along.

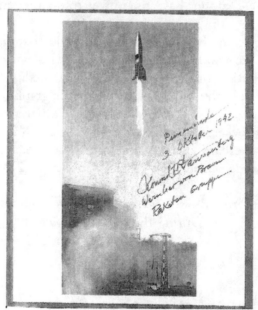

First ever rocket launch of the A4—
known as V2—October 3, 1942.

The work at Peenemünde led to everything from manned space flight and satellites, to remote control technology for rockets and planes, Scud missiles and drones. Technological advances that led to the Space Shuttle originated at Peenemünde. Computer chips and cell phones also were eventual by-products of work begun at the rocket facility.

Unfortunately, my father and other specialists also produced the rockets that rained havoc on London in the waning days of the war. At Peenemünde, the rockets were known as the A4, but to the world at large they became the V2 after *Vergeltungs Waffe* or Revenge Weapon.

What's more, nearly 20,000 slave laborers died working at Peenemünde and at the underground manufacturing plant in Lehesten, Thüringen—many more than were ever killed by the rockets the facility produced. Did my father and his colleagues know about the workers and the terrible conditions in which they existed? Maybe. Did they have the power to do anything about it? Probably not.

According to my father's colleague, Werner Baum, my father was *the* man because he was able to eliminate one of the key problems of getting a rocket successfully launched. He suggested they use graphite in the rocket rudders because graphite would not melt or break up under intense heat. This and other breakthroughs led to the first rocket launch ever on October 3, 1942.

Bernhard Gerhardt was married once before. His wife had committed suicide, leaving her husband to raise a 12-year-old son, Heinz.

They lived across the street from Christa von Hitzeroth whose store sold fine linens. During the day, Heinz was left on his own

My parents at the beach with sister Gitta and brother Guenther.

while his father went off to work. Christa took a liking to this friendly, well mannered but sad-looking child who had lost his mom.

Heinz began telling his father how nice Fraulein von Hitzeroth was and how much he liked her. That led to a meeting, and after a short courtship, they married. These were the years after the Great Depression, and I am certain the wedding included only a small circle of family and friends. But my father had a job. The pay was not great but it was a job—and an exciting one at that.

I was born Hans-Joachim Gerhardt in Peenemünde in December 1941 in *die Siedlung*—the village—where most of the rocket specialists and their families lived. I was the youngest of four children and everyone called me Hansi.

My half-brother Heinz was 21 years older than me; sister Gitta, six years older; my brother Guenther, eight years. There was another brother, born two years before me, but he died of heart complication shortly after birth. I don't know if I was expected or not but I was lovingly welcomed.

I wasn't even two when Peenemünde's cover was blown, and on the full moon night of August 17, 1943, the Royal Air Force's Operation Hydra launched 596 aircraft to bomb the rocket center. The bombers mostly missed their target. Perhaps the facility's glass roofs mirrored the sky and the sea. Stories circulated that when air raid alarms sounded, powerful submarine engines flooded the concrete areas between the buildings, adding to the disorienting mirror effect that may have confused the bombers.

However, falling bombs did kill a thousand civilians. Our family hid safely in shelters during the attack, but others who decided to stay home were killed, including a close friend, Dr. Walter Thiel, the deputy director. Most of the village was destroyed. We relocated to a Schloss or manor house owned by the von Braun family at Buggenhagen, 45 minutes from Peenemünde.

I have three vague memories of the Schloss. My first memory is of chasing a turkey until the turkey decided to chase me, and I ran screaming into my mother's arms.

Another memory is of my father arriving home from one of his many travels in his chauffeur-driven silver-grey Opel. The Opel had a shiny chrome grill which fascinated me. I remember moving my head in its reflection, watching with delight as my nose grew to enormous proportions and then shrank again.

The third memory is much more frightening. The war must have been coming to an end, as I remember seeing Russian tanks emerging from the woods behind the Schloss, knocking over the big fountain in the driveway before continuing on towards Peenemünde.

My memories of the end of the war are equally fragmented. By the time those Russian tanks crashed into our water fountain, my family was scattered. Brother Heinz had become a soldier in the war, lost a leg and was hospitalized in Prague, Czechoslovakia.

My father apparently had been assigned to hide documents when he was arrested near Lehesten, Thüringen and interrogated by a special U.S. Intelligence commando group known as Operation Paperclip. When the Russians seized the area, he was turned over to them and sent off to Russia. That was the last our family heard from him.

With my father missing and my mother hearing horror stories about how the advancing Russian army was treating German civilians, we decided to flee the Schloss, managing to board the last freight train headed west. My sister Gitta, my brother Guenther, and my mother packed everything they could manage into my stroller—I was three at the time—taking some jewelry and leaving everything else behind. The train headed for Hamburg. We did not care where it went as long as it took us west toward the Allied armies, away from the much-feared Russians.

We were finally dropped off at a refugee camp north of Hamburg, and then eventually transferred to Itzehoe, 60 kilometers north of Hamburg in the province of Schleswig-Holstein. As we moved around, we shared apartments with local residents. They disliked being forced to share their homes with strangers and we didn't like it a whole lot, either.

Two years later, we got our own home at Feldschmiedekamp 53, two rooms on the ground floor of a very old, shabby house. The toilet was an outhouse. A passageway was our "washroom" because that was where the only faucet was located. No one occupied the living room—we had no furniture, and couldn't afford to heat it. Hard-to-find cardboard helped insulate door panels and keep out blowing snow.

Beside the coal-fired stove were two beds, one for my mother and sister, and one for my brother Guenther and I. We soon found a farmer who took my mother's jewelry in exchange for food and straw to stuff our makeshift beds. Any twig we found became fuel. I still have a scar on my forehead where I was hit while attempting to steal coal from a steam locomotive— evidence that I made a lousy thief.

Most food was rationed—butter, milk, meats—but there was always a farmer with whom you could barter food for jewelry or cash. I certainly appreciated any luxuries such as milk, butter, eggs, and fresh fruits. Certain bakers added sawdust to enhance their bread's weight. Real coffee was not available unless you had money to buy it on the black market. Residents in the area kept chickens and goats. Neighbors grew vegetables on their balconies.

Across from us lived two women whose husbands, a father and son, were sailors in the German Merchant Marine. Whenever they came home, the whole neighborhood knew it. They brought American cigarettes, real coffee, chocolate, and lots of alcohol. Within days of their return, fights broke out, the husbands accusing their wives of infidelity; the wives accusing their husbands of the same thing. Furniture flew through windows. When father and son tired of fighting with their wives, they fought with each other, employing sword-like knives picked up in Holland to cut cheese wheels.

These knife fights would flow from the house into the street, stopping what little traffic passed by on the narrow road. It was all pretty harmless in the end. Little blood was spilled, and nobody ever got really hurt. On a sober day the father and son would rest, sharing stories of their world travels. I was fascinated. Maybe it was those stories that years later sent me off in search of adventure at sea.

Toilet business was done during daylight hours. At night the rats took over the outhouse. Even in daylight, you stomped your feet while perched on the potty. Every two weeks, a horse-drawn wagon would arrive. Workers in leather aprons and shoulder pads emptied the outhouse into iron buckets. They then carried gallons of waste on their shoulders from the outhouse to the street, leaving a trail of residue behind. The neighborhood stank for days after these collections.

Electricity, like the gas, was coin-operated. You bought coins at the local grocer's and then put a token in the meter in our washroom. One coin was good for 20 minutes. You never left the lights or the stove on unless you really needed them. When you left one room, you turned out the light before you entered another—no big deal since we had only two rooms.

There was little work available immediately after the war, but my mother found a part-time job cleaning the local fruit and vegetable store. While she came from an educated background, she now cleaned floors. I never heard her complain. She could provide for us, and to her, that's what counted—nothing else.

Everything was so scarce, not only food and clothing, but also raw materials. I collected and sold nails, pieces of wire, cans, scrap metal, anything I could get my hands on. If you made a dime or even a quarter, you felt rich. Imagine how much candy that could buy back then! Our part of West Germany was under British control (later handed over to the Danes), and while we were recent enemies, it seemed to me as a kid that we actually liked each other in many ways.

The soldiers would share a pack of chewing gum or pass a cigarette to a parent. I collected cigarette butts and gave them to a neighbor who smoked them in his pipe. American cigarettes sold for a premium on the black market. This was as close as most Germans came to smoking one.

At the age of eight, I was fortunate to get a job as a part-time delivery boy for the local fish store. Big tanks in the store were filled with trout, eel, and carp, a north German specialty. Making my deliveries earned me my first real money. I had a ready smile and pleasant attitude—a precursor of things to come—and I even made good tips.

As I made my rounds, I was shocked by the number of deformed and mentally challenged children I encountered, hidden away by parents ashamed to have the neighbors see them. My deliveries also frequently took me to older people who lived alone. Waiting to be paid, I inspected photographs and portraits hanging on the walls—invariably, a husband or son who had failed to return from the front, mainly Russia.

Soon I became involved in a second business. A large washing powder company sent out flyers that could be redeemed for a free sample at the local grocery. One of the employees from our grocery store gave me a couple of samples and told me to knock on doors, collect the vouchers, and give people the powder sample. For doing this, I got paid 25 Pfennig, not a small amount in those days. It wasn't long before I started sub-contracting this work to younger kids. At one point, I had four employees delivering soap samples.

Immediately across from us was a repair shop, Feldschmiede Anders, that for 100 years had shoed horses and repaired cars. The Anders were rich enough that they were able to purchase one of the first Mercedes cars built after the war. Their son Rainer, ten-years-old, was the same age as me, and a good friend. He was able to drive his father's big trucks as long as he stayed on their property. However, when the new Mercedes arrived weeks went by before his father allowed him to sit behind the steering wheel.

One Sunday, Rainer showed me the car. Together we admired its fine lines, big lights, chrome bumpers, and wheel hubs. He then carefully opened the driver's door and invited me to sit on the passenger seat. Turning the key, he started the engine and put the car in reverse. Next, he shoved the gearshift into forward, moving the Mercedes slowly up the driveway and then down again.

In awe, we exited this amazing car. Walking away, we turned for one last admiring glance. That's when we realized the car had not stopped. In fact, to our horror, we saw that the Mercedes was still moving!

Rainer, the ace driver, had neglected a minor detail. He had exited the car leaving the gearshift in neutral, forgetting to pull the parking brake. The car rolled elegantly down the sloping drive, headed onto the street where neighborhood kids were playing soccer. It swooped through the front gate, picking up speed, like a movie in slow motion. Frozen to the spot, we watched as the car crashed through the big showroom window in the furniture store across the street.

I can still hear the booming voice of Herr Anders behind us, *"Was ist hier passiert?"*—What happened?

We just stood there, too scared to move. Without another word, he grabbed both of us by the scruff of the neck. I could have sworn we were airborne as he swept us into the garage where he proceeded to administer each of us a truly memorable spanking.

Chapter Two

For years, it was just my mother, brother, sister, and me, together—the four of us fighting to survive the hardships of life in postwar Germany. We had no idea what had happened to my father after he disappeared. But my mother never gave up hope that somehow, some day, he would find us.

She heard of wives who wrote to Russian leader Josef Stalin and on occasion those letters led to the release of imprisoned German husbands. But the 1940s became the 1950s and still no word came.

Then one day in April 1951, a letter arrived from the new West German government. It said my father had been found and that we would be reunited with him shortly. A couple of weeks later, we were told he would be back around noon May 11.

I always wondered what my father looked like. All I could remember, really, was that he had one arm. Other than that, I had no memory of him. There wasn't time to even grab a photograph when we left. Since then I had not even considered the possibility that he might some day re-enter our lives.

So while there was great excitement in our household, I was nervous and not keen to meet him. When I saw his car arrive, I ran over to Anders garage and hid. My father came looking for me, but it was my mother who finally persuaded me to come out of hiding to meet him. He embraced me but I could not bring myself to do the same. He was a stranger and now I had to share everything with this man: our home, our food, not to mention my sister and brother and my mother.

Walking back to our apartment, he had put his arm on my shoulder and he tried to get a conversation going. But all the time I kept thinking, since he only had one arm, was this his prosthesis on my shoulder? Where would he sleep? Was there to be no more bedtime conversation with my mother if she was sleeping with *him*? That first night, dad slept in the front room on an old couch someone donated. Mother continued sharing her bed with my sister. But there was no denying dad was back, and things were not to be the same.

I remained curious about his prosthesis. I asked him to take it off and he did. This rather heavy thing became an occasional play toy for me since he seldom wore it around the apartment because of the weight. He was never a man of many words. He enjoyed an occasional cigarillo-type cigar, but he hardly ever drank and disliked socializing. His only real love was soccer, a love he shared with Guenther. Curiously, they never would sit next to each other at a game.

It was not easy for my father to fit in with our family or society in general. A war had been lost along with a prestigious job. A once proud man who walked straight and tall, had now somehow become small and bent—hardly surprising considering what he had been through these past five years.

From what I was able to discover later, once he was arrested and interrogated by the Americans and then turned over to the Russians, my father, along with 270 other rocket specialists, was taken at gunpoint to Russia. Once there, they were divided into 10 different research camps.

The Russians had been slow to embrace rocket technology, but when they discovered what the Americans were up to, they were

*German rocket specialists and families celebrate Easter
at the Russian prison camp in 1949.
My father is third from right.*

anxious to move ahead with research, employing the talents of my father and the other captured specialists. My father's camp was located in Khimki near Moscow. It numbered 17 inmates, including such rocket specialists as Werner Baum, Oswald Putze, and Willi Schwarz.

The Khimki camp inmates were tasked with redesigning the A4 engines. They also developed engines that eventually were used in the ICBM missile and the Soyuz space rocket. The Russians always denied that the Germans did anything for their rocket program. But when Stephan and I attended a 2006 conference at the Technical University of Dresden, Germany, to commemorate the 60th anniversary of the German rocket specialists in Russia, there was ample evidence of German inventions that were still being used in the Russian space program.

Their usefulness finally at an end, the Russians began to send the captive specialists back to East Germany. My father was released in October 1950 and returned to Lehesten in the East German sector. He escaped in February 1951 and got to West Berlin with the help of British Intelligence. Werner Baum, the team leader in Khimki, also escaped to West Berlin and was held by the British for weeks before being released. He would later find a job with Siemens in the turbine engine design. Still alive in his 90s, I call him every other month at his home near Frankfurt.

In Berlin, my father again fell into the hands of the Americans before finally being freed. That's when he came home to us. By that time, he was not well. The Russians warned him that if he ever discussed his work for them, he would be killed. Therefore, he never talked about his captivity. It was only years later that I discovered details of the life he had lived in Russia, a life that included a relationship with a German-Russian interpreter named Ilse Neumeister. They had a son together.

In 2007, I found Ilse Neumeister's daughter, Stefanie Kropp. Both Frau Neumeister and my father's Russian son had died; the son in 1954 and Ilse Neumeister in 1983. Curiously, her daughter only discovered in 1985 that she had a brother. The mother never said anything while she was alive. Part of the continuing mystery of my father.

Just how he got back to us was another mystery I have never fully solved. I am still searching for debriefing notes from either the U.S. or the British government, trying to find out more.

Once my father entered West Berlin, what happened to him for the 10 weeks he was held by the Americans? Did he go to the U.S. before returning to Germany? Perhaps. Werner Baum told me they were both offered jobs in the U.S. with Wernher von Braun's rocket team. However, they were denied permission to emigrate. American authorities considered them communist "implants" because they thought their escape from the Russians had been "too easy."

I never had much of a relationship with my father after he came home. At least he and my brother Guenther shared a love of soccer. We didn't even have that together. He was even more disappointed in me when I showed no interest in engineering.

I was more like my mother, always smiling, enjoying people, wanting to learn new things in new places. My mother as a young woman had lived in Hungary, spoke the language, as well as a bit of French and English. She had no problem communicating with people. I wanted to be like her. I had no desire whatsoever to be like my father.

Our relationship finally blew up one day over, of all things, dice. He was attempting to explain their mathematical dimensions for a school project I was doing. I was bored, paying scant attention. Abruptly, he lost his cool and despite having only one arm, he smacked me on the nose. I went reeling back in shock, my nose bleeding. This would happen each time I disobeyed, he angrily announced. My father had hit me before but never like this.

Something happened between us that day. It became clear to me that we were not going to get along.

It was time to leave. I was 15 years old.

My parents 25th wedding anniversary, 1958

Chapter Three

As soon as school ended in 1957, I got a *Seemanns Buch*, a license to work on ships. Once I had this, I moved out of the house so that I would not change my mind—or have it changed for me. Was this the right decision? The stories spun by the father-son sailors on our street, not to mention care packages from relatives in the United States filled with chocolates, canned food, and clothing, only encouraged me to escape what I viewed as my stifling existence. Out there, somewhere, was a better life. I decided I would go and find it.

How did my father react to all of this?

Nothing.

He showed no emotion when I announced my decision, but I believe he must have been sad, having lost his last chance to influence any of his children's education. My mother just wept. She was the one who traveled as a young person and told her children about a wider world out there. Still, she was sad to see the youngest leave.

But then my mother, the eternal optimist, always encouraged me to dream. She saw what I saw, a great world to conquer. Even so, I had to promise her over and over again that I would be careful and write once a week.

I was all set to go, but naturally I was fearful. I was only 15, after all. What lay out there for me? My friends were impressed. I was escaping. They were stuck in a small town where nothing ever happened. I was the lucky one. But as I left home, I wondered.

Arriving in Hamburg, I stayed at the Stella Maris Seaman's Mission. A teenager, away from home for the first time, I was desperate to blend in—and more scared than ever.

That first night, sleeping in my bunk, I was awakened by the arrival of my roommate, a very drunk Norwegian sailor. He had been robbed and beaten on the *Reeperbahn,* Hamburg's famous red light district. Even though he was covered in blood, he assured me he was okay and immediately fell into a deep, drunken sleep.

I never slept for the rest of the night.

The next morning, I made my way to the busy common washroom and managed to find a free wash basin. As I reached for my toothbrush, I spotted a glass eye rolling across the counter, quickly stopped by a giant hand. A booming voice erupted from a towering sailor, minus one eye. He peered down at me and growled, "Watch it, kid."

We later became friendly and he showed me the scar on his head where they had installed a platinum plate, a souvenir from a bar brawl in Amsterdam. This one-eyed giant was only one of the fascinating characters staying at the hostel. You had to be careful and keep an eye on your belongings as many of these sailors were between jobs, beset by financial problems, and eager to "borrow" just about anything from your toothpaste to your money.

It took me four weeks to find a job as a cabin boy on a 5000-ton freighter, MS *Harmonia,* licensed to travel between Germany and the European coastlands, including the Mediterranean. Our first voyage took us to Finland where we loaded lumber bound for Syria.

We embarked from Hamburg at the end of May 1957. We steamed along the Elbe River into the northeast canal between the North and Baltic Seas. Entering the Baltic Sea, the weather remained calm. The chief steward and I were in charge of looking after the captain, the first and second officer, the chief engineer, and two others. I was new to the ship and untried at sea, but no matter, I was up for the job.

Then the weather turned. The wind came up and the ship started to roll. Before I quite realized what was happening, I became seasick. Cigarette smoke (I had started smoking myself but quickly stopped), greasy food, and various kitchen odors did not help. I turned white and became deathly ill—much to the delight of the seasoned crew. What's more, I couldn't sleep, kept up half the night by the sound of breaking ice crashing relentlessly against the hull of the ship.

The weather worsened. Waves grew to monstrous proportions, lifting our vessel high out of the water and then bringing it crashing down again with a force that literally made it shudder. Steel plates moved like rubber. I was petrified and, on occasion, so were some of the roughest, toughest sailors on board.

Finally, the weather calmed, and we arrived safely in Oulu, a seaport northeast of Helsinki, Finland. As soon as we dropped anchor, the ship was boarded by customs officials. There was prohibition in Finland, Sweden, and Norway, so liquor was like gold. The old sailors had stashed booze on board planning to use it as barter for sex. A few ladies' men employed rum as after shave.

One of our crew members, knowing we would be inspected, used a fishing line to lower a net full of booze from his cabin porthole. The customs officials knew that trick and soon discovered his loot. Nonetheless, we had a lot of female visitors, eagerly plied with liquor and American cigarettes in exchange for sex.

Leaving Oulu, we entered the Mediterranean via the Strait of Gibraltar, an awesome sight. At the seaport of Latakia, the principal port city in Syria at the eastern end of the Mediterranean, we loaded barley bound for Denmark before moving on to Beirut, at the time one of the world's most beautiful cities, "the Paris of the Middle East."

Tripoli, the capital of Libya, our next stop, had to be more discrete when it came to providing pleasure. Returning from a sightseeing trip in the desert, our driver stopped at an oasis for gas. We were escorted into a large tent where women lounged about waiting to service weary travelers. It was human trafficking at its worst. These poor women had to oblige any camel driver who wanted their services.

The manager of the establishment, realizing we were German, had a special treat for us—a scarred and tattooed German prostitute. We were shocked; how in the world could one of our countrywomen get stuck in this hell-hole? We paid the guy a couple of bucks to go away so we could talk to her.

She told us that she had met her Libyan fiancé at school in Germany. He convinced her to come to Libya to meet his family, except there was no family. Once in Tripoli her passport disappeared, and the Libyan sold her into a life of slavery. She was traded a couple of more times until she was not "good enough" for a household and was reduced to working in this whorehouse.

We offered to help, contact her parents or relatives, but she declined. It was better that they believed she was dead. She was too ashamed to go home. We took down her name, the city she was from, the university she attended, and the name of her fiancé. Later, we told the story to our local shipping representative. This was a common tale in the Middle East, he said. By the time authorities were able to investigate, the women usually had disappeared.

For the better part of a year, I traveled the world. I was the untried kid, often the butt of practical jokes, made to work very hard serving fellow shipmates. I was in awe of my surroundings—being on the sea at night with no land in sight, no pollution, seeing the most glorious stars filling a black sky.

I saw Mount Vesuvius spew lava, witnessed a Greek oil tanker and an English freighter that had collided in a heavy fog burn into the Bay of Biscayne, and helped transport two injured crew members onto a tiny U.S. Coast Guard boat bouncing around like a cork in heavy swells along the eastern coastline of the U.S. I held my breath while propane tanks lashed to the deck came loose and plummeted into sea, fearing at any moment we all would be blown into eternity. In Malta, a British submarine emerged from the water and almost hit us.

I experienced all sorts of storms at sea but the most unusual occurred close to the Egyptian coastline. The first hint of what was to come came when the alarm rang. We were ordered to close all windows and doors. Outside, sweeping across the water, a huge red cloud rolled towards us—a sand storm at sea! It was over almost before it began. However, the fine sand got into everything and seemed to stay with us forever.

Filled with these images and many more, I arrived home for the first time since leaving in January 1958. My mother, of course, had written many letters and I, of course, had written none.

Finally, she wrote to the shipping company. Thereafter, I was ordered to write her a letter or postcard at least once a month and show the ship's captain the evidence. After mom died in 1984, I found all my letters from that time in a file. I guess she missed her baby boy and must have read those cards and letters over and over again.

After nine months at sea, working seven days a week, I took leave from the ship for a well-deserved vacation. I arrived by train late at night and then walked home with my suitcase. The door flew open after numerous rings. Instead of my parents, an outraged stranger glowered at me. He yelled that he had no idea what had happened to the Gerhardts but they no longer lived here.

Only then did I vaguely recall that my mother had written to say they were moving to another part of the city. Fortunately, a neighbor out late walking his dog, remembered where they had relocated. With no taxi in sight, I walked another seven kilometers and finally found them. There were lots of hugs and kisses from my mother. Even my father seemed happy to see me, yet, as always, he kept his emotions in check.

Naturally, I bragged to my buddies about my seafaring exploits,

Visiting Gitta in Canada, 1959.

the amazing waves, the incredible sights, the unusual foods. Seeing my friends working or studying, with girlfriends and family, made me realize there was something to treasure in this small town—something a wandering life at sea could never give me.

Six weeks later, I was on board another ship, the MS *Learina*, this one bound for Canada where my sister Gitta lived. The Atlantic crossing was difficult. We found ourselves lost in a fog among huge icebergs and with no radar—our system had broken down. The telegraph officer, thankfully, was still able to send and receive messages via Morse code. That enabled him to get some information about the location of the icebergs. Nonetheless, all hands were on deck keeping a watch. We stood there in the freezing night, eyes glued to the ocean as bells clanged and fog horns moaned, signaling any nearby ships that we were in distress. Eventually, we managed to thread our way through the ice and get ourselves into safe waters.

When we reached Canadian shores, we encountered a new water system of locks, canals, and channels, the St. Lawrence Seaway, allowing ocean-going vessels to travel from the Atlantic to the Great Lakes. We just missed Queen Elizabeth who had presided over the opening ceremonies on board the yacht *Britannia*.

My first stop in this curious country I'd heard little about and never visited was Baie Comeau in Quebec. As soon as we came into the harbor, we were visited by three German immigrant families desperate to purchase dark rye bread. It was among the many things Germans could not find in their new country. They worked in the Canadian mining industry and did relatively well—driving around in big American cars, a sure sign of prosperity as far as I was concerned. I will never forget being invited for a drive in a big light blue Chevrolet Bel Air, the one with the big V-shaped back. What an automobile!

I found my sister working in Toronto as a secretary at Fairweather, a Canadian women's clothing company with head offices in one of the North American high-rises I had heard about but never seen. Toronto was full of them.

Later, traveling between Hamburg and Chicago with the Hamburg-Chicago Cargo Express line, I visited Gitta often. My mother was delighted that we had connected across the ocean. I even had photographs to prove it! I told my mother of the strange customs in Canada: on Sundays everything shut down, no sporting events or movies, no liquor. Eaton's and Simpson's, the largest department stores in town, actually draped over their display windows. At the same time, there were these big cars, wide roads, and clear blue skies—so very different from Germany.

Chapter Four

In those years, I traveled the world with a Hamburg-based company, Ahrenkiel and Behne, working on different types of ships. The largest was the *Amelie Thyssen*, a 35,000-ton coal and iron-ore freighter. We regularly crossed the Atlantic to pick up coal from Virginia bound for Amsterdam or Rotterdam.

Coal, as you might imagine, is a dirty business. While you try to keep everything locked and sealed, coal dust creeps in everywhere. The loading of a coal ship was fascinating to see. Locomotives on shore pushed a wagon filled with coal down a ramp. When it picked up enough speed, the wagon rolled up another ramp and then down along a separate track where it came to a stop directly in front of our ship. Then the wagon was plucked up by a crane-like system, lifted into the air and turned upside down, dumping coal into the hold.

One of our voyages took the *Amelie Thyssen* to Arkhangelsk, known in English as Archangel. The city perched on the edge of the White Sea in the far north of Russia. Entering Russian territory was a problem since one of our sailors had raised the Russian flag upside down, a sign of distress and disrespect. In retaliation, the Russian Navy searched us from top to bottom, confiscating all our western reading materials.

Life was obviously very difficult for people living there. The extreme temperatures did not allow proper road paving, and huge wooden planks in the tundra formed the main road to the city. Sitting in a rundown Opel bus left over from the German Army— the swastika still visible on the doors—my head hit the ceiling every time the wheels struck a board sticking up on the road.

We made our return trip via Kirkenes in Finland on the Barents Sea. Where is Kirkenes? When you round the north cape, you make a sharp right turn and there, between Russia and Norway, is that sliver of Finland. During the Second World War this was a German naval base. One of its unique features, a tourist attraction today, was an underground bunker that could hold 9,000 people, virtually the entire population of the town.

Heaving under the weight of a full cargo of iron ore, we headed out to sea again. In those days, you checked for leaks in the cargo holds with a weighted line lowered down pipes to the bottom of the ship. To our horror, we discovered that we had taken on 250 tons of sea water in one of the forward holds, making us top heavy. This was very dangerous—a wave could crash over the bow and with the weight in the hold, bring the ship's bow down. A second or third wave could send the ship straight to the bottom.

Immediately, the alarm went off, an SOS signal was sent, and we were on standby with life vests on, expecting to go down at any moment, knowing that in these icy waters, we wouldn't stand much of a chance.

However, luck was with us. NATO maneuvers were taking place not far away. Soon we were surrounded by fighter planes and warships, escorting us at slow speed into the harbor at Bodoe, Norway where divers soon discovered that several bolted metal plates had come apart. The bilge pumps became clogged by iron ore dust and failed to work.

At the ripe old age of 17, I was reaching the conclusion that the life of a sailor was fraught with danger. We entered the port of Aqaba, Jordan amid tracer fire whizzing toward the Israeli town of

Eilat. We couldn't get out of there fast enough. Going through the Suez Canal you could see sunken ships at the bottom of the canal, their masts sticking out over the water line. The same was true in Norway, where we had to maneuver around sunken World War II vessels as we entered port.

Frequently, returning to home port, we found the police waiting to arrest my shipmates on charges that ranged from robbery to murder. Our cook was charged with killing a gas station attendant with a brick after he broke into the station. One of my bosses was taken away, charged with child molestation. Scary, but this was life at sea. All sorts of craziness went on.

One of the stewards I worked for spit in every cup before serving it. He also discovered that munitions from starter pistols could blow clay ashtrays apart. He loved that. On a voyage to Galveston, Texas, he bought two guns with holsters. He made me balance beer bottles on the ship's railing and then ordered me to call "Draw!" As soon as I did, he drew his guns and shot at the beer bottles—with real bullets! Unfortunately, he was a terrible shot, and would either miss his target or hit the railing causing bullets to ricochet, nearly hitting me. No fun. I declined his invitation to try it myself.

It must have been much easier to buy guns in America than whiskey because soon everyone on board our ship seemed to be packing heat. One time, I was called to clean a toilet late at night. I heard gun shots and encountered two drunks in the midst of a gunfight, actually firing real bullets at one another.

I yanked the fire alarm. An officer came running and confiscated the guns. The two gunmen were furious with me for turning them in. They got their revenge several weeks later. After smoking a lot of *hobbli bobbli*, a type of hashish bought in the Middle East, they grabbed me and tried to toss me into the Indian Ocean. Luckily, another sailor came by and stopped them.

Another time, a crew member became angry because I could not open the liquor store room when they ran out of booze during a party. Later, when I poked my head into the crew mess, the angry

My last voyage aboard MS Learina.

crewmember spotted me and heaved his *malspieker*, a tool used to scrape rust off the ship. It whizzed past, missing my head by an inch.

I was beginning to tire of it all, the danger, the drunks, the filth, cockroaches as big as your fist, the bad weather. I had wanted freedom. Now I began to wonder if I had too much of it.

My last voyage took place in February 1960. We were transporting a cargo from Hamburg bound for Maracaibo in Venezuela and from there on to Turbo, Columbia, where we would take on a load of mahogany trees.

When we got to Turbo, barges carrying the mahogany came alongside our ship. The trees were then lifted into our holds. We could take motorboats into port only during daylight hours— floating logs and other debris could sink the boats after dark. For good measure, the river was full of man-eating piranhas. If you went ashore, you were there for the night, no matter what happened.

Life in Turbo was primitive. The only electricity came from generators. There were no roads and no real buildings except for a few huts and two bars that were actually whorehouses.

Ten of us came ashore and, of course, ended up in the bars.

I was 17 at that point and still a virgin, a fact I should never have revealed to my fellow shipmates.

They pooled their money and hired a hooker to bring a screeching halt to my virginal state. All 300 pounds of her would be employed in order to reach this goal. She dragged me to her room, literally shooing the rats away. Once inside, she set about seducing me. What with the rats running along the top of the room divider and the weight of my seductress, nothing worked as it should. After a while, she got tired of trying and let me go, my virginity still intact.

I stumbled out to discover everyone was drunk and occupied with other ladies of the night. I had to go to the bathroom, so I went through a back door and climbed a rickety ladder to an open pit used as a lavatory. Next to the pit was the bar's generator.

As I stood over the pit, one of the other crew members appeared, a loud-mouthed Berliner named Atze. He took one look at the generator and started fooling round with it, pulling at the lever that shut the engine off, plunging the bar into darkness.

The last voyage: farewell to the sea.

That brought several unhappy Colombians, screaming at us in Spanish. Atze yelled at me to get out. But where to? Before I could stop him, Atze yanked at me and we both jumped down into the pit, landing in a sea of smelly shit full of curious things slivering along its surface.

Our assailants, unable to believe we were stupid enough to literally jump into a shit hole, departed.

Atze and I managed to climb out, filthy and stinking, swearing as we made our way to the harbor, intending to clean ourselves off. Then we remembered the piranhas. Neither of us dared stick so much as a toe into the water.

We stumbled to another bar where we were greeted like lepers. However, after cash changed hands, we got a room to clean up and some used clothing. I had nightmares for a long time afterward. Atze, however, seemed totally unaffected.

That was pretty much it for me. By the time we got back to Hamburg, I'd had enough of the sea. I had decided there was a safer way to make a living.

Or so I thought.

Chapter Five

I loved walking through the grand hotels of Hamburg. There were two that were famous, the Vier Jahreszeiten, Four Seasons Hotel (no relation to the Four Seasons Hotel chain), and also the legendary Atlantic Hotel. Both were located at the inner city lake, Die Alster. As I walked through the hotels' grand lobbies, I envisioned myself in a fancy uniform, welcoming famous guests from around the world, and serving delightful meals prepared by three-star Michelin master chefs.

Maybe, I thought, a career in hospitality would be exciting, and perhaps it could take me out of the poverty and hard living I had known and get me to the more refined places in the world—places I had yet to experience but desperately wanted to see.

Unfortunately, the kind of hotels where I dreamed of working were not hiring, at least they weren't hiring young, untried former cabin boys like myself. Rather than being unemployed, I worked for six months in the shipping department at Gruner & Jahr (now Bertelsmann, one of the world's largest book publishers and printers). However, I was determined to get into the hotel business and soon found a job as a waiter at a small country inn belonging to Otto Count zu Rantzau, related to the House of Hohenzollern, the German royal family.

When I started there, the inn, Die Breitenburger Fähre, served stranded travelers awaiting the incoming tide to take them across the Stör River (today there is a bridge). Fortunately for the count, the inn was just one kilometer away from his castle. I was hired as the house waiter which meant that when tourist buses arrived from Denmark at six in the morning, I was hauled out of bed to hoist a case of beer onto my shoulder and carry it to the thirsty Danes for "breakfast."

You delivered the beer, collected the money, and then went up to get another case. I must have walked hundreds of kilometers working for that inn. Die Breitenburger Fähre occupied the most beautiful setting imaginable by the Stör River. Wednesdays, government offices closed at noon. It was known as *Beamten Nachmittag*. Guests came from the city for *Kaffee und Kuchen*, coffee and cakes.

As their waiter, I had to trudge half a kilometer from the inn to tables beneath the willow trees, ask guests what they wanted, and then walk back and deliver the order. I learned quickly to ask the right questions, remember the answers, and always carry matches along with postcards of the inn. I also learned to deliver coffee, keeping it warm and not spilling it.

Our coffee was legendary. Ninety-year-old grandmother Oma Nagel, the owner's mother-in-law, made sure the water was tested every spring and fall. This had been going on for generations. The local coffee roaster would spend hours with her blending the coffee beans and roasting them to perfection. Huge earthen urns were used to make the coffee. It was good for only 45 minutes or so.

"After that, its flavor changes," Mrs. Nagel maintained. She would not allow it to be sold. She was right, of course, which is why we had so much repeat business.

Count zu Rantzau's family had fought for generations with the kings of Denmark over the lands between Denmark and Schleswig Holstein, the most Northern state in Germany—where those famous cows originated. After every storm the count would walk the dykes winding along the Stör River with his staff and the farmers leasing land from him, checking for damage caused by icy winter winds.

Count Otto was a man in his early 50s, almost indistinguishable from the farmers, wearing a similar green *loden mantel*—a warm coat—rubber boots and a wide brim hat with a feather and a piece of deer antler attached to the side.

After hours braving the icy winds and rain atop the dykes, the count and the farmers often ended up back at the inn. I would place a bottle of the count's specially-blended rum on the table, marking a line on the bottle. Whatever was drunk would then be charged to his account.

Steaming hot water was mixed in a stem glass with the rum and a sugar cube—grog, a wondrously powerful beverage to help the count and his minions thaw out after the dyke inspection. The count was known for his ability to consume goodly amounts.

As much as I enjoyed working at the inn, I felt I had to move on with my life and career. I began an apprenticeship at the Dithmarscher Hof, the finest hotel in Itzehoe. Since the inn did not employee a maître d' or someone with a master's degree in the profession, my time there did not count toward my apprenticeship.

Thankfully for me, the hotel possessed a life-changing force by the name of Eugen Christian. He may have been only five-foot, six-inches tall, but Eugen, always immaculately dressed and a wonder to behold, was a giant to me. No one in the business influenced my life more than he did.

Eugen was educated and trained in 1920s Berlin at the world famous Adlon Hotel, directly across from the Brandenburg Gate. In that era, the Adlon was the most luxurious hotel in Europe, if not in the world. Eugen, or Mr. Christian as I would call him, told how the staff was lined up each day at the start of their shift to ensure hair was properly cut and washed, fingernails cleaned and cut, shoes shined, teeth brushed. No heavy perfumes were allowed. Albert Einstein, Marlene Dietrich, Charlie Chaplin, and Josephine

Baker, were among the guests who enjoyed amenities such as towel warmers and heated marble bathroom floors.

Eugen had an interesting past. He was married to Gerda Christian, who became Hitler's secretary in 1937 and stayed with him until the end. Soon after his marriage, Eugen left his job at the Adlon to become an air force officer. Eventually he headed Hitler's advance team, in charge of organizing the Führer's schedule.

Not surprising, perhaps, the job and the politics were not to his liking and he soon wanted out of Hitler's team and his marriage. That did not go over well either with Hitler or his wife.

The Nazis tried to kill him in 1944. He came home one night and a team of assassins—he always assumed it was the *Reichssicherheitsdienst*, the Führer's personal security force—opened fire on him. They missed but years later his 90-year-old mother could still show us where bullets lodged in the door of Eugen's house.

His many talents included an uncanny ability to throw his voice. For example, preparing to serve duck, he would have a conversation with the guests. As he talked to them, he would throw his voice, making quacking sounds across the room where I was standing, sending me into fits of laughter.

We had a wonderful relationship. I admired him as a boss and as a mentor who taught me the finer points of service, personal hygiene, respect for the guests, and the guest's territory. He also taught me discipline and reminded me constantly never to forget why you are here and who is paying your wages and tips. Good staff members are seen but not heard, he said, unless they are spoken to or are offering service.

Know your food and beverages, Eugen said. Listen and remember details, especially names of guests. That was particularly good advice. Remembering people's names in life did not just bring good tips, it was good for business in general. I learned to look at guests and to listen but always have a sense of what is going on in the room, and never stand with your back to a guest. Today, good manners remain the gold standard of fine service.

The work at the Dithmarscher Hof was hard. I started with breakfast service at six o'clock in the morning and then lunch. A couple of hours were free in the afternoon, but then it was back to work at six o'clock until the last guest had been served late into the night.

Our owner, Heinz Gruber, came from an old German hotel family that for generations owned a hotel in Dresden, Saxony. He ran his Itzehoe establishment in the manner of a grand hotel, bringing master chef Franz Hindl from East Germany. Franz would make the star of TV's *Hell's Kitchen* look like a pussy cat.

Yelling and screaming while at the same time preparing food that was not great, he became a one-man reign of terror. Once I had the audacity to return a burned veal cutlet. He screamed at me to mind my own business and then threw a chopping knife at me. The knife missed, bounced off the stainless steel counter, sailed through a foot-wide window in the service door, and then shot down the stairs striking a guest in the back. Luckily he was wearing an overcoat and was not hurt.

And I thought life at sea was dangerous.

On another occasion, teaching one of our kitchen apprentices how to skin a rabbit, a waiter said something. Immediately, Franz turned and whacked him across the face with the bloody skin, spraying blood over his white jacket and shirt. The waiter went screaming out the door in front of astonished hotel patrons, never to be seen again.

This sort of behavior, amazingly enough, did not get the chef fired. However, when Franz discovered one of the apprentices sleeping with his wife, it took nearly the entire kitchen staff to keep him from killing the apprentice right there in the kitchen.

That, finally, was the end of our master chef.

A prominent surgeon in Itzehoe, Professor Lohse, was a pioneer in the science of rebuilding human veins. Some of the richest men in the world visited the professor. These wealthy patients stayed in our hotel for three to four weeks before surgery and then for two to three weeks afterwards.

Many of the professor's clients were from the Middle East. Being away from their ultra-conservative homelands sometimes brought out the worst in these multi-millionaires and even more so from their entourages, given that their employers were in hospital for extended periods. The doctor's clients would arrive in chauffeur-driven Cadillacs. One Cadillac came outfitted with Persian carpet floor mats as well as solid gold door handles, grills, and bumpers. The chauffeur thought nothing of daily driving 120 kilometers to pick up French newspapers.

One Saudi Arabian sheik's bodyguards, burly, unsophisticated men with too much money to throw around, imported prostitutes from nearby Hamburg. Drunken orgies ensued, including hallway races with naked hookers mounted atop room service carts. Having spent time in many Middle Eastern countries and seen the intense poverty and the strict Islamic religious rules, the spectacle of these men carrying on the way they did made me furious. However, there was nothing that could be done. We were there to serve the customer, after all.

Chapter Six

In the summer of 1963, I was working at a small resort on the
Baltic Sea when a phone call came from my brother, Guenther.
Our father had died in his sleep. A stroke.

My parents' marriage was strained after the war. Still, my father's
death deeply affected my mother. Whatever their problems, she
had lost her lifelong partner. My brother and I were saddened.
The war, his captivity in Russia, his reduced circumstances back in
Germany had changed him, and he could never warm to us and
be a real father.

My sister Gitta flew in from Canada and we had a small
funeral. Afterwards, as was customary, there was a wake. My father
never drank very much. It was hurtful to see people supposedly
celebrating his life getting drunk, something he would never have
done.

Gitta and I escaped to pick up our half-brother, Heinz. He
arrived by train from East Germany where he had been living since
the war. It had taken him three days to get the appropriate papers
to attend his father's funeral. I was a baby the last time he visited
Peenemünde, 20 years before. East-West politics had prevented
us seeing one another. My mother, however, stayed in touch with

him, writing letters, so we knew he had married a nurse and had a daughter, Ute, and a son, Michael. The family lived behind the Iron Curtain in Leipzig, Dresden and later in East Berlin.

When the train arrived, we looked at every passenger coming up the stairs at the railway station. We almost gave up hope when we spotted a man limping along, carrying a wreath and a small suitcase. He passed us, and we both called out, "Heinz!"

He turned around and it was indeed our long-lost brother, much older-looking than a man in his mid-40s, but almost identical to our father. It was eerie burying our dad and a couple of hours later meeting his twin.

Having lost his left leg during the war, Heinz had finished his studies and become a locomotive design engineer for the East German government. Life was difficult in the East. After *Die Wende,* when the two Germanys were reunited, Heinz often wondered how his life would have been in the West. Later, he would visit us in Canada and we saw him and his family several times. Sadly, he died of prostate cancer shortly after Ralph and I visited in 1994.

I was a waiter when I met a lovely-looking young lady named Helga Manske. I had noticed her at our weekly jazz night at the Harmonia Club, but I was shy. A third year apprentice in the fashion department at Karstadt, Itzehoe's largest department store, she thought I was the funny guy always telling jokes.

We finally met when she and her colleagues from work came for a snack at the hotel. I started to flirt with her. She seemed impressed with how I juggled a number of dinner plates at the same time while serving her and her friends. We knew from the beginning—with a little help from our friends—that we had something in common. Even so, it was a couple of years before we actually started to date. After that, things moved quickly. Less than a year later, in January 1964, we were engaged, and then married in May.

Helga never met my father, but I certainly had the pleasure of meeting hers. The pleasure was not reciprocated. His advice to his daughter: "Stay away from hairdressers, musicians, and waiters."

That definitely included me. He consented to our marriage because he thought I got Helga pregnant, and was expecting grandchildren. He would have to wait a couple of years.

We had a lovely wedding on a beautiful day in May 1964, perfect except for the fact that my father-in-law almost burned up my car driving us to city hall with the parking brake on. As the wedding ceremony began, I was a bit distracted, staring out the window, watching smoke pour out of the automobile.

When the justice of the peace asked if I would take this woman as my wife, Helga promptly interjected, "Yes he does!"

A sign of things to come?

No sooner were we married than we moved to West Berlin. The German capital until the end of the war, Berlin in 1961 was a city occupied by the Russians, French, British, and Americans, situated in the middle of what otherwise was Russian-occupied East Germany. On August 13, 1961, the Russians built the wall that infamously divided West Berlin sectors from East Berlin.

The West German government was anxious to repopulate what it thought was an aging city. Therefore, all sorts of tax incentives were offered to anyone who decided to relocate. It also exempted young men from the draft. That did it for me. I did not want to join the military. Berlin, here I come!

Whatever the pluses of the city, easy affordable accommodation was not among them. After paying an agency a stiff fee, we finally found a room in one of the large old Berliner apartment buildings. It was one room. We shared the bath with four other residents.

Helga took one look and was in tears. The place was dirty, noisy, and far from home. Still, it's amazing how you adapt, no matter the circumstances. We went to work cleaning the place, decorating as best we could, and getting to know our neighbors.

One of our fellow residents, an elderly gentleman, knocked on our door as soon as I left for work each morning and asked Helga if he could borrow salt, sugar, a cigarette, anything he could think of. We suspected he had more on his mind than a cup of sugar.

Next door lived two men and an Indonesian woman. If we read the noises from their apartment correctly, the three of them shared everything. When they were not making love, they got into loud fights. Only after Helga and I along with other residents began complaining did they settle down.

Another neighbor was a bachelor who nightly entertained his hooker girlfriend. They were into bondage. You could hear the crack of a whip and her moans. Helga was sure he was beating her. That may have been true, but she seemed to enjoy it.

After a time we got used to the craziness and actually began to enjoy ourselves. This was our new home. It could even be quite romantic beneath the giant chestnut tree in the inner courtyard where, every Sunday, a harmonica player put on an impromptu concert. If you had a request you wrote it on a piece of paper, wrapped it around some coins, and threw it down to him. People leaned out of their windows and sang along, applauding the music, happily waving greetings to their neighbors.

Mitzi was the building's caretaker, a tiny, hard-working woman of indeterminate years who liked a drink. Whether she was taking the trash down four floors, firing the boilers with coal, or washing the stairs, she was usually drunk.

Our landlady constantly destroyed Mitzi's booze stashes in the basement coal bin and begged everyone not to give her liquor. However, our resourceful caretaker still managed to find a drink. Mitzi, in short, was a true Berliner, and we couldn't help but like her.

Berliners always reminded me of New Yorkers. They tend to be loud, fast on their feet, with a good sense of humor, and, when it counts, a heart always in the right place.

Helga found a job in the ladies fashion department in one of Berlin's biggest and most prominent department stores, Kaufhaus des Westens. Everyone called it Ka-de-We. My job at the Hilton Hotel Berlin was minutes away.

The Hilton was the city's newest and most popular hotel.

Every room had a shower, if not a bath, unusual in those days. The Rotisserie dining room was among the best in town, and thus was filled with celebrities attracted to Berlin by the post-war movie boom.

Standards at the hotel were extremely high. For example, you could not write down the orders unless there were more than six guests at a table. Anything less, and you had to remember what guests ordered. Everything was served on heavy silver platters,

We worked in teams of three, overseen by an assistant maître d' who helped with the flambés as well as table cooking and carving. Our clients tended to be educated diners and could be very fussy and snooty. They expected only the best and usually got it.

In the year I worked there, we experienced everything from a murder-suicide (a Swedish millionaire and his male lover) to the hotel controller jumping off the roof. The controller had been having an affair with one of the apprentices. When the hotel discovered their affair, he was fired. He had a final drink at the bar and then went up to the roof and jumped. He flew down past a restaurant packed with startled diners.

For a young man like myself, the hotel was a place of constant excitement and glamor at a time in Europe when excitement and glamor were hard to come by.

In 1965, the western comedy movie *Cat Ballou*, with Jane Fonda and Lee Marvin, premiered at the Berlin Film Festival (Marvin, won the Silver Bear for his performance). The celebration was held at our hotel where the ballroom was turned into a western saloon. Everyone on staff was outfitted in cowboy costumes, except me. I had to stand by the door in fancy tails, grey pants, and a purple jacket with silver stitching along the collar.

Lee Marvin came in happy, a little drunk, but scorning the fancy-looking drinks being served. He promised to give me the brass sheriff's badge he was wearing if I could find him his drink of choice, a super-sized glass of tequila, straight up. I managed to get him his drink, and I still have his sheriff's badge.

Berlin in those days may have been the world's most fascinating city. To imagine what it was like to live there, you must build a wall around the city where you live, cut it off from the rest of the country, if not the world, and then divide it in two with a wall that slices through houses, gardens, streets, and lives. Now add spotlights, barbed wire, and heavily armed guards, and you have some idea what it was like in Berlin in the 1960s.

The wall was impossible to miss or ignore. Low-flying Russian fighter jets highlighted the ongoing tension between East and West. Life was punctuated with news of the frequent, often deadly attempts by East Germans to flee to the West. They did this in many wildly desperate and inventive ways—everything from building kites, hiding in cars and digging tunnels, to swimming land-mine strewn waters and jumping from apartment buildings.

Any kind of communication between East and West was difficult. People living in the Eastern sector of Berlin needed a special passport. Families could only get together by waving at each other from either side of the border. Eventually, the East German government even put a stop to that.

Travel from West Berlin to West Germany was a challenge since one first had to drive through East Germany. Rigorous inspections of every automobile and its passengers were standard procedure. After being visually inspected by heavily-armed guards, you proceeded through a zigzagging maze to the inspection center. Steel beams and concrete blocks on wheels were in readiness to stop any vehicle that tried to escape.

Your car was inspected with mirrors rolled underneath the body. The gas tank was measured, luggage opened. The amount of cash you carried, once declared, had to be counted in front of an officer. Any magazines or newspapers were confiscated. Passports were shoved into a slot beneath a mirrored window, inspected by an official you could not see. Forms had to be filled out detailing the exact contents of a car, who was in it, as well as the destination in the West and the purpose for going there.

One time it turned out I had two more Deutsche Marks in my

wallet than I had written on the form. The guards made me get out of the car, walk around to my wife's side, and give her the money.

The route between Berlin and your destination was exactly timed. If you arrived too early at the next checkpoint, you automatically received a speeding ticket since the speed limit was 90 kilometers an hour and they could judge how fast you were going.

It was worse to be late traveling between checkpoints. If you were delayed even slightly, the immediate assumption was that you had stopped and contacted East Germans and might be helping them escape to the West. Your car was then taken apart.

Once a friend and I crossed the border in a tiny car with no trunk, although the hood was designed so that you might think the trunk was in the front. When a female border guard demanded to know what was in the trunk, my friend replied, "When I sit in the car, it's my feet."

I started to laugh. Big mistake. Immediately we were pulled over and then taken to a garage where East German authorities proceeded to tear the car apart. We spent hours there. No more jokes after that.

The scariest journey was also my last trip through East Germany. By this time we had decided to immigrate to Canada. A colleague agreed to give us a lift to Itzehoe in the West. We loaded the car with as many of our personal belongings as we could squeeze in. Helga ended up in the rear, hidden by a wall of boxes.

It was a foggy night when we arrived at the border. The guard at the first checkpoint appeared like a ghost out of the mist. The normal questions were asked: "Where to? Why? Personal or business? How many people traveling?" We handed him three passports but apparently the guard did not see Helga in the back. Therefore, he reported to his station that only two people were in the car.

At the next checkpoint they found three people when they were expecting two. All hell broke loose. More damning still, I had U.S., Canadian, and West German currency in my possession. Hours of interrogation followed while Helga and my friend waited outside. I was held in a drab office, questioned by an officer and two soldiers, everything recorded on a big two-reel tape recorder.

They wanted to know who I knew in the East and in the West; why was I moving to Canada and why then did I have U.S. currency. As time went on, I began to worry they weren't going to release me, that I was finally trapped behind the Iron Curtain.

They suspected the personal belongings we packed into the car were actually merchandise intended for sale. Therefore, I would need the proper transport documents. After all this, we were forced to turn around and drive back to West Berlin. Waking the landlord in the middle of the night, we carried our belongings up three flights of stairs back into our apartment.

The next day we mailed all the items we could to West Germany and then rented a car, drove to another checkpoint, and crossed without difficulty.

Thank goodness for the West. Freedom at last!

Nearly 25 years later, I happened to be in Italy when the wall that haunted my early life, and the lives of so many Germans,

People from around the world gathered at the
Brandenburg Gate.

finally came down. I tried to reach my brother in the East. It took days but finally we connected, and I flew to Berlin. I had only 20 hours before my next appointments in London, but I didn't want to miss this historic moment.

My colleague Hartmut Zunk, general manager at the Kempinski Hotel, understanding why I was in Berlin, put me into the presidential suite. My brother Heinz could hardly believe it when he arrived with his wife Elfriede, son Michael, and his sister Ute, her husband Ulli, and daughter Kirsten. They had never seen such luxury. Later, I packed up all the amenities in the suite, including bathrobe and coat hangers, and gave them to my family, asking Hartmut to charge me. He never did.

I asked Heinz what kind of food he and his family would like to eat. Italian, they promptly answered. There was no Italian food behind the Iron Curtain. The concierge made a reservation at one of the best Italian restaurants in town. The owner himself escorted us to our table. Everyone enjoyed the food. The night filled with laughter and the sounds of a family remembering.

When it came time to pay the bill, I offered my American Express card. The waiter whispered that they only accepted cash. I excused myself from the table. All six of my fellow dinner guests followed me with wide eyes as I approached the owner and arranged to have the bill charged to the hotel. Everyone looked noticeably relieved when I returned. Charging meals were unknown in the East. They were sure the evening would end with everyone washing dishes.

We walked together over to the Brandenburg Gate where thousands of people had been gathering for days. TV networks from around the world rented every available crane so they could lift their cameras over the remnants of the wall. Young and old hugged one other and drank champagne. It was truly an historic moment in our lives. Standing at 3 a.m. on top of the wall, shaking hands with people from around the world, I thought what beautiful times lay ahead; peace for everyone! It was not meant to be, of course. But for one blissful night, anything seemed possible.

*A peek from West into East Germany through a
hole chiseled in the Berlin Wall.*

Chapter Seven

Partially because I'd always wanted to speak French, Helga and I decided to move to France. In 1965, I actually applied for a transfer and was hired at the Hilton Orly Airport Hotel. But then my sister Gitta convinced us to immigrate to Canada instead.

We applied for our papers at the Canadian Consulate and were fortunate that we had a relative in the country. We received our visas within seven weeks. Almost too fast. Now what? Did we really want to leave Germany? The decision was complicated by the fact that Helga was pregnant with our first son, Stephan.

Still, Canada's housing was plentiful, and I already had lined up a job prospect. We decided to go for it. Helga's parents were in shock. First she married a waiter, then he took her to Berlin, hours away from Itzehoe, and now—Canada? We dared not tell them about the pregnancy; they already had enough to deal with.

After a few hectic days in Itzehoe, we made our way to Bremerhaven and boarded the SS *Berlin*, an old passenger liner on its last voyage before it went to the scrap yard in Italy.

On November 20, 1965, we found ourselves in the middle of the stormy Atlantic bound for a new life and a new land. An old

SS Berlin

sea hand by now, I'd weathered many storms, but the crossing was not easy for the pregnant Helga. I ate most of my meals alone in the dining room and brought room service back to Helga.

We arrived in Montreal on December 3 and boarded the overnight milk train to Toronto. In those days it truly was a milk train, slowing at villages and towns en route to pick up milk cans on station platforms.

The train finally chugged into Toronto's Union Station on a rainy grey morning. Gitta and her husband Rudolf were there to welcome us. They drove us to our new home, a flat my sister had rented for us in the Casa Loma area. Rather sparsely furnished, it nonetheless featured a welcoming bed. We instantly fell asleep understanding that Gitta would pick us up for dinner.

Around five o'clock, I was awakened by a strange ringing. I sat up, thinking someone was at the door. I opened the front door, but no one was there. The ringing continued. Eventually, I found a white phone on one of the book shelves. A telephone! We did not have such a thing in Germany; no television either.

I picked up the receiver and in good German fashion announced my name. Gitta, meanwhile, put her phone down next to the radio. A male voice said, "This is Eddy Luther, flying over the Don Valley Parkway. Traffic is very heavy." Believing that I talked to a real person, I ask him to please slow down. "It is my first day in Canada."

Obviously, it was going to take time to adjust to life in this new country.

My first interview resulted in a job at a downtown Toronto hotel called the Walker House. The oldest hotel in Canada at the time, the Walker House was a simple railway hotel where people paid in cash, had no phone or TV, just a clean bed.

It would have been torn down were it not for a former World War II colonel named Doug Crashley, stationed in Germany after the war, who fell in love with the country. As a result of that experience, he and several well-to-do war buddies decided to create Canada's first European-themed restaurant complex.

Working with well-known architect John Meikkeljohn, they opened a number of spots inside the Walker House Hotel, including the Swiss Bear Lounge with 400 seats, the Rathskeller with 275 seats, and the Franz Josef Supper Club with about 200. Later, they also operated what became the first discotheque in Canada, Grannies.

The restaurant complex was an instant success. Line-ups formed

I am on the right in the Rathskeller advertisement.

on the weekends. My pay was 85 cents an hour, and I worked 20 to 25 hours a week. Initially, those working hours alarmed me. We had come to Canada with only a few hundred dollars. A baby was on the way. I would need more income than that. However, I soon learned of something unique to North America: tipping!

The tips added substantially to my income. What's more, many of the older waiters did not want to hang around when things were slow and often gave me their shift. My good nature and professional training were quickly rewarded with great tips from the guests. Within five months, I was promoted to assistant maître d'.

There had never been anything in Toronto quite like the Walker House. The elegant Franz Josef Supper Club with its crystal Swarovski chandeliers, silk wallpaper, and hand-crafted chairs from Austria, gave the impression that you had entered a genuine Austrian fine dining establishment.

Tuxedos during the week and tails for the weekend were standard uniform for the maître d' and his assistant. Captains, waiters, and busboys wore burgundy jackets with white shirts and black bow ties. The kitchen brigade under chef Ted Linden, later chef Fred Reindl, created sumptuous meals, elegantly served by a well-trained staff that was mostly Austrian or German.

Tableside cooking was a specialty and all the rage in those days. Everyone was going crazy for flambé. The bigger the flame, the better the tip. I think back on those times with horror and relief that we didn't set someone on fire.

During this period I met the man who was to become a great friend and one of the legendary characters in Toronto newspapers, Doug Creighton. Red-haired, with a merry twinkle in his eye, Doug would help found the *Toronto Sun* and become its publisher. But when I first met him he was editor of the *Toronto Telegram*, a feisty newspaper fighting for its life against competition from the *Globe and Mail* and the *Toronto Star*.

The maître d' introduced me to Doug as the "new" waiter, Hans. Doug's guest was another regular who later became a wonderful friend, George Gross, sports editor of the *Telegram*. George was Czech but spoke fluent German and helped me with Doug during our initial conversation.

Doug ordered his usual luncheon drink, a double martini on the rocks with a twist of lemon. He wanted to know about my family, where I was from in Germany, how long I had been here. He was immediately warm and welcoming. However, he did make one thing clear to me; I must tell the chef that under no circumstances was I ever to serve him anything with nuts. He was deadly allergic to them.

Walker House Hotel reunion: from left: manager Peter Hackenberger,
owner Douglas Crashley, Chef Fred Reindl, me, and
Toronto Sun *founder Douglas Creighton.*

Doug often stopped in for dinner and the show. One night his waiter recommended the mulligatawny soup, a classic Anglo-Indian specialty with diced chicken and chicken stock, cream, cumin, curry, and a spoonful of long grain rice sprinkled on top with almonds.

The room was dimmed, ready for the show to start, when

Doug's soup arrived. He picked up his soup spoon. I spotted Doug from across the room and casually asked the waiter what he had ordered. The mulligatawny soup, the waiter replied. I turned and saw to my horror that Doug was about to take the first spoonful.

"Mr. Creighton! Don't eat that soup!" I screamed across the room.

Doug immediately dropped the spoon. Not only did Doug not touch his soup, but as Doug recalls it in his memoirs, neither did 150 startled dinner guests.

Walker House general manager George Schwab and manager Peter Hackenberger with actress Marlene Dietrich.

Chapter Eight

While I struggled to build a career, working a split shift five or six days a week for lunch and dinner, learning the language, and getting used to the Canadian lifestyle, Helga had her own challenges. Very pregnant, and also learning the language, she had to run a household, do the shopping, and take care of life in general.

Fortunately, we had Gitta living not too far away. Stephan was born in April 1966. I always joked that he was made in Germany and born in Canada. Fourteen months later, Ralph was born. Helga spent many evenings alone while I was working. Not having a car in the first year, we either traveled with my sister and brother-in-law or via public transport. Contrary to Germany, Sundays were the quiet days in my business. Laws prohibited serving liquor, there were no sporting events, and most businesses in general were closed.

A major snow storm at the beginning of May 1966 made us wonder if winter ever ended in our newly adopted country. Hot and humid days in July and August also were a major change for us. After a while, though, we not only got used to all the changes and challenges but also started to enjoy life in Canada; a very different place from Germany and very different today compared to the 1960s.

A year after I started in the Rathskeller, I was promoted to assistant maître'd in the Franz Josef Supper Club by my new boss, Hans Kocaurek. We made a good team and a lot of money. Both of us had sunny dispositions, liked to take care of people, and possessed a great memory for names.

One of our regulars was the president of Mercedes Canada, a real character named Rainer Lange-Mechlen. He was a very bright man who loved the Walker House and would bring his entire executive team in once a month.

We became friends and one evening ended up at his home in Oakville, outside Toronto, talking through the night. At one point, he went to his safe and brought out a small box. "I rarely open this," he said, "but tonight I want to share something I cannot forget."

He explained that during the Second World War he was a young student pulled out of university and forced to join the military. He was trained as a pilot.

Rainer opened the box and showed me an Iron Cross, the highest honor in the German military, the equivalent of the British Victoria Cross. Then he pulled out various other items including insignias given to him by enemy soldiers.

In an aerial dog fight when an enemy fighter was shot down, the plane's tail number was recorded. If he could, Rainer, as was the custom, tried to find out what happened to the downed pilot. If the pilot survived and was taken a prisoner, Rainer visited him, and that's when they exchanged pieces of each other's uniforms.

Years later, working for Mercedes in the early 1950s, he oversaw establishment of the company in the United States. Since Mercedes was just starting up in the U.S., he knew just about everyone who bought one of their cars. Driving through Manhattan one day he saw a parked Mercedes with a missing hub cap. He stopped and left his business card on the windshield with a note to contact him and receive a new hub cap compliments of the company.

The next day he had a call from the car owner. "Lange-Mechlen, you son of a gun," the caller said. "If you think a free hub cap allows you to get away with shooting me out of the sky, you're crazy!"

It turned out the owner of the Mercedes had faced Rainer in a dog fight and been shot down. Rainer had visited him in hospital. Not only did the downed pilot get a new hub cap, but he and Rainer stayed friends for the rest of their lives.

Supposedly we celebrated with champagne;
it was really ginger ale in a Dom Perignon bottle.

The Ascot Inn, a hotel opposite the Woodbine Racetrack near Toronto's airport, was yet another acquisition by Walker House owner Doug Crashley. George Schwab, the general manager of both operations, gave me the opportunity in April 1968 to become a maître d' at the inn.

Built at the suggestion of Crashley's friend, the billionaire business tycoon and race horse owner, EP Taylor—he also happened to own the nearby racetrack—the inn featured a charming Swiss-style lobby, banquet facilities, and 110 rooms. Overlooking the Humber River Valley, it made it an ideal hideaway at the city's edge.

As the Iron Kettle Restaurant's new maître d', I soon attracted a number of my downtown clients such as Doug Creighton, Gerd Stoppenbrink, president of Kühne + Nagel, and Rainer Lange-

Mechlen. We had a great executive sous chef, Aldo Aglio, who could not do enough to please guests. As a result, our little restaurant quickly became known around the city. A year after arriving, we were voted the best restaurant in Toronto by the prestigious Holiday Traveler, and I received the Ambassador Tourism Award.

Despite the awards and the success that came with them, the Ascot Inn attracted its share of trouble, mostly because it was so close to both a racetrack and a major airport.

Racetrack gamblers arrived to celebrate their wins or mourn their losses. Businessmen seeking afternoon assignations appeared to account for a large portion of our occupancy. The parking lot turned out to be a convenient dumping ground for stolen cars used by bank robbers flying into Toronto from Montreal.

Ernie, the assistant manager, offered services not listed in our brochure. "Would you like a room with or without company?" he would inquire of single male guests.

Ernie kept a stable of ladies available on short notice. Rick Knie, our manager, put a stop to that. Word spread that this "service" was no longer available and neither was Ernie.

After a while, though, I looked at our clientele a little suspiciously, particularly anyone who was a big tipper. Who knew where the money came from?

Len Casey of Ontario Place pins on my
Toronto Ambassador Award medal.

If I thought life in the hotel and restaurant business would be safer than going to sea, I was sharply reminded that my new profession also had its share of perils.

When two guests wanted to know more about the inn, I ran to get them a brochure. I'd traveled all over the world, survived the roughest seas, the most dangerous waterfront bars. Yet when I reached the top of the stairs at the Ascot Inn, I slipped and flew into the air before landing hard on my right elbow, shattering it in several places. I was rushed to hospital and required surgery. I finally recuperated after five months of daily physiotherapy.

Even dealing with the staff could be hazardous to one's health.

One of our chefs was a good cook but a mean-tempered racist who loved to throw pots and pans at people. The situation was not helped by the addition of a Moroccan-Jewish waiter and a Jordanian waiter who brought to work their homeland battles and prejudices. The cook sided with the Jordanian waiter. A scalding hot metal tray was taken from the oven and left out for the Jewish waiter. As soon as he touched the tray, he realized how hot it was and dropped it. That was enough for him. He told me he was quitting immediately.

I persuaded the waiter to stay and reprimanded the cook. The Jordanian waiter started calling me names behind my back. Finally, enough was enough, and I fired him at the end of his shift. He attacked me with the four-inch blade of a corkscrew knife. I have never seen, before or since, a person so full of hate. Only after we called the police and he was threatened with arrest and deportation, did he cool down.

Scary, but then life tended to be like that at the Ascot. Just when you thought it was quiet, everything running smoothly, something happened.

By now I had become assistant banquet manager with an office off the lobby. One day I overheard the desk clerk take a call requesting immediate help in room 112. No one else was around, so I went to see what the guest wanted. I arrived at the room and knocked a couple of times. No one answered.

Finally, I used my master key, opened the door and stepped into a scene of horror. The white bedspread was drenched in blood. A nearby phone, also white, was similarly blood-soaked.

Yet the room appeared to be empty.

I stood there in a state of shock. Then I heard moaning sounds coming from the closet. I went over, opened the door and found a man lying on the floor soaked in blood, his hands and face bleeding. Thankfully, he was still alive.

I called for an ambulance and he was rushed to hospital. The story of what happened to him was so bizarre it was hard to believe.

A test pilot for an airline manufacturer, his plane had crashed during a test flight, severely burning his legs. After being treated at nearby Humber Hospital, he had checked into the hotel. Full of painkillers, he nonetheless had a few drinks in our bar and then ordered a dozen beers from room service. For some reason he decided to place the beers in the closet.

As he was doing this, he dropped the tray full of beer. Some of the bottles exploded, and he fell on top of them, slicing open his face, chest, and hand. Bleeding profusely, he crawled across the room to the phone to call for help. Then for some reason he made his way back to the closet again. That's where I found him.

In the hotel business, I was learning that one cannot make this stuff up.

Chapter Nine

A star is born.

In 1972, the Hyatt Regency chain was about to open a spectacular hotel in downtown Toronto. At the time it was the most exciting development in the hotel industry, ushering in a new era for a city suddenly awash in places for visitors to rest their weary heads.

Between 1972 and 1975, in addition to the Hyatt Regency's 540 rooms, the Four Seasons Sheraton opened up 1,450 new rooms. The downtown Holiday Inn and the Westin (now Hilton) each added 600 rooms. The Harbour Castle (now a Westin Hotel) opened yet another 800 rooms while the Prince Hotel (a Westin property) added another

500. As well, during this period several smaller hotels opened for business.

But all eyes were on the Hyatt Regency. After opening their first Hyatt design in Atlanta, the company grew hotels like mushrooms. The design was unconventional—huge atrium lobbies became a Hyatt signature, as well as state-of-the-art rooms, unique indoor-outdoor swimming pools, convention facilities, stand-up bars, and high-end dining rooms such as Truffles.

The new Hyatt Regency was located on Yorkville Avenue, an area in the midst of transition from its counterculture roots into high-end boutiques and restaurants. For good or ill, the Hyatt became part of that transition.

Frans Schutzman, an eloquent world traveler and gentleman, was the general manager. I met him on several occasions when he came to dinner at the Ascot Inn. He encouraged me to apply for a job with the hotel.

As it happened, my former boss from the Walker House Hotel, Hans Kocaurek, and the executive chef, Fred Reindl, had already started working at the Hyatt. It was a good fit all the way around, and I was hired as the director of catering in December 1971.

How do you open a new hotel? Carefully, and with great attention to detail, because the speed accelerates from zero to 100 overnight. Forgetting something simple, like ordering spoons or plates or linens, gets you into big trouble. Every day gets busier. There is never enough time.

Everything was ready to go when I arrived—even the sales and marketing teams were in place—however, the hotel was still under construction. Entry was only possible wearing a hard hat, not exactly an enticement for our guests.

Little and big things were not quite right. The pre-opening brochures did not do the hotel justice. What's more, the ballroom seating calculations were wrong. The numbers of patrons who could be seated had been over-estimated by as much as 80 percent.

When I brought this up, no one believed me. Not until I rented a couple of tables and chairs and set them up in the unfinished ballrooms was I able to convince everyone mistakes had been made. I thought I might be fired. But the reaction was just the opposite.

Once the storm died down, it became apparent that the kid, me, had established some credibility with the team.

As the deadline for the hotel's March 15, 1972 opening grew nearer, we all worked crazy hours. When a young woman called inquiring about the bridal suite I asked her for how many? She hesitated before she whispered, "Two?"

After a long day, my colleagues and I would sit down for a late dinner and have a drink. Sometimes two. A staff member got drunk one night and insisted on driving home. We grabbed him and as a joke rolled him into one of the huge rolls of carpet ready to be installed the next day. We then forgot about him and he fell asleep.

The guy woke up in the middle of the night, found himself trapped in a huge roll of industrial carpet, and screamed blue murder until the night watchman found him. He didn't drink so much after that. We decided not to roll any more employees up in carpets.

On the day the hotel was to open, we realized at one o'clock that we had yet to receive a liquor license. Our lawyer, Trevor Eyton, volunteered to go to the Liquor Control Board of Ontario and apply for it. He came back waving the permit and by six p.m. the hotel's SRO bar was full of guests celebrating the opening of Toronto's most exciting new hotel.

However, the holder of the hotel's liquor license was not in fact the hotel but one Trevor Eyton. He remained the permit holder for many years, long after he had become CEO of Brascan, the real estate corporation.

The gala opening featured Count Basie and his orchestra playing for guests invited from all over North America. The hotel was an immediate hit. Truffles Restaurant, with its real gas lanterns, beautiful Italian fabrics, Royal Doulton china, Riedel crystal glassware, and elegant silverware, brought fine dining in the city to a new level. The themed uniforms for the well-trained international staff, the Italian maître d', Sandro Julita, and later our Spanish maestro, Emilio Calderone, didn't hurt either. We had a terrific team and many of them went on to even better things.

Rooms manager Antoine Corinthios became president of the prestigious Four Seasons Europe-Africa-Middle East division. Franco Prevedello, the banquet manager, became one of the hottest restaurateurs in town and is now a successful condominium developer.

Roy Whiston, the head bartender at the SRO Bar, is retired and lives around the corner from me. We still get together for coffee. Ian Barbour was the assistant maître d' at the rooftop Odyssey Bar and Restaurant. Years later, we were at a fund-raising dinner together. Someone asked how Ian and I met. At the Hyatt Regency, I said. I turned to Ian. "Did you leave before or after me?"

"Before," Ian smoothly replied. "You fired me."

Oh.

Frans Schutzman shows comedian George Jessel his cuff links,
a gift from President Nixon.

The man who oversaw the whole operation, Frans Schutzman, was, hands down, the best hotelier I ever worked for. He had his moods, certainly, but he was a great professional. I'll never forget when he spotted a match lying on the floor in the lobby. Quickly, he stooped to pick it up and then handed it to a passing bellman. "Deposit this in the next waste basket, please."

Thereafter, my head did a 360-degree spin whenever I saw him coming, scanning the floor to ensure I did not miss a match or anything else.

"This is our hotel but we are in the guest's territory," he would say. "Treat the hotel like your home and pay respect not only to the paying guests but also to your co-workers."

That's a lesson I never forgot, and he was so right. Mr. Schutzman, as most of us called him, spoke six languages, was always impeccably dressed and coiffed so that he looked like one of the hotel's wealthy guests. In fact, he traveled the world and dined with kings and presidents.

He told amazing anecdotes about working at the legendary Raffles Hotel in Singapore in the 1950s. While there, Mr. Schutzman, knowing the British author Somerset Maugham was nearing the end, invited him to stay at the hotel one last time. In his writing, Maugham had helped make the hotel the international byword for, as he put it, "all the fables of the Exotic East."

Yet when the Bank of China, the hotel's new owners, got wind of the invitation, they objected. Mr. Schutzman still wanted Maugham at Raffles. An invitation, after all, was an invitation. He paid for Maugham's final stay out of his own pocket.

Ironically, Schutzman later established a Somerset Maugham suite at the hotel. No objections from the Bank of China once the author was dead.

Naturally, the popularity of the new upstart Hyatt Regency was not viewed happily by competitors, notably the Park Plaza across the street, run by a man named Ed Shaughnessy. One day, Mr. Schutzman invited Mr. Shaughnessy for lunch. With a wicked sense of humor that apparently was absent in Mr. Shaughnessy, Mr. Schutzman assured his guest that he had the best view in town. Suspicious, Mr. Shaughnessy inquired as to why. "Well," said Mr. Schutzman, "you are looking across the street at our beautiful new building!"

With that, Mr. Shaughnessy got up and left. He never spoke to us again. Which is not to say we didn't hear from him in other ways.

For example, we organized a cocktail reception and hotel tour for taxi drivers, the people who would be driving guests around the city and to and from the airport. The reception must have been a huge success for soon after Mr. Shaughnessy found himself in a cab back from the airport, growing more irritated each mile as the driver sang the praises of the fabulous new Hyatt Regency Hotel.

The angry Mr. Shaughnessy worked his considerable clout, and city council passed a bylaw prohibiting drivers recommending a hotel or restaurant unless asked.

Being part of the team opening a new hotel is hard work. Anyone interested in a career in the business should have the experience. However, I'm not sure I would want to go through it again. There are so many things that can go wrong, so many initial miscalculations that can come back to haunt—from design mistakes, construction delays, staff and equipment shortages, to outright theft

Design errors at the Hyatt became the most blatant and, alas, most enduring of those miscalculations. Here's an example of what I'm talking about: because of cost overruns, individual dimmer switches inside the ballroom were discarded. It was a small thing but a huge mistake.

When we had a presentation in the ballrooms, we had to add a telephone inside each section so the technician manning the main dimmer rack could be called. The technician then had to flip multiple switches, one at a time, to produce a desired lighting level. This was complicated and time consuming. Customers complained that our system for lowering the lights was stupid and had to be changed. Unbelievable that an architect could have deleted such a small but integral part of a hotel's lighting.

One of the sales features we pushed during the Hyatt's construction was   I cringe even thinking about it—shag carpeting. It was featured throughout each guest room, including the bathrooms, and even extended into the hallways. That did not last long. Soon after the opening, we had to replace all the bathroom carpet with tile because it was just too unhygienic. We later had to do the same with the shag in the bedrooms.

An expensive but valuable lesson: today's fashion is always in danger or becoming tomorrow's design horror. I still have nightmares featuring endless miles of shag carpeting.

Chapter Ten

It's one of the enduring mysteries of my professional life: what is it about a hotel that inspires people in distress to spend their last night on earth in an anonymous room?

One morning I was walking from floor to floor checking for room service carts. By this time, I had been promoted to food and beverage director. As I came onto the fourth floor, a man in his late 40s dressed in slacks, bare foot and shirtless, came screaming out of his room. "I don't want to die," he yelled. "I don't want to die!"

Blood gushed from his left wrist where he had cut himself open with a breakfast knife. Startled, I grabbed his wrist trying to stop the bleeding. He continued to cry out as he sprayed me with blood. Finally, I pulled the nearby fire alarm and then continued to hold him until help arrived.

He survived, but we never heard from him again. The police reported that the man was from Toronto, had gone through difficult divorce proceedings, and lost his job. This happened a lot. You would help someone in distress, save their lives in many cases, and never hear a word from them, no thanks, nothing. I suppose they were embarrassed and found it easier to pretend that nothing had happened.

One Monday morning I was asked by the convener of a Canadian insurance convention to check a delegate's room. The delegate had attended a cocktail reception the previous evening but had not been seen since.

The duty manager and I opened the door to the room and found a man in his 50s lying dead on the bed. A towel was draped over his left thigh, his lower body turned dark blue where blood had collected. Not a pretty sight.

When the police and coroner arrived, they agreed the deceased had suffered a heart attack. They further agreed he suffered the attack while receiving oral sex provided by a prostitute. That was, I thought, a lot to deduce from looking at a dead man lying on a bed, but I was only a hotelier. What did I know?

A month later we received a call from the dead man's widow. She accused us of stealing a suit of his and demanded its return. We finally found the suit in lost and found. What with her threatening phone call, I was tempted to tell her what really happened but in our industry, discretion is key.

We apologized for the oversight and sent flowers.

The most heart-rending hotel suicide I encountered involved a young couple in their late 20s from Buffalo. Overweight and not well dressed, they arrived with a one-year-old baby boy in a beat up old car. Their credit card cleared enough to cover a two-day stay.

However, food and beverage charges, along with parking and phone charges, soon raised a red flag. The front office manager asked the couple to explain how they would settle their account. Our credit manager also got involved but by this time it was the end of the day. We would follow up the next morning.

Some time that night, apparently driven by the bankruptcy of their lighting business, they took an overdose of sleeping pills. The wife died but the husband remained conscious. When he desperately phoned the hotel switchboard, a quick-thinking security guard and night manager got the husband to hospital. They found the baby still alive, lying on the bed beside his dead mother.

When I came in the next morning, I found my assistant, Wendy Bannon, with the baby. A little while later, the Children's Aid Society took the child away. Everyone involved in the incident was saddened and hoped that somehow this cute little baby boy would grow up in a strong and loving home. The husband did recover. He wrote us an apologetic letter.

The things people would do inside a hotel never failed to astound me. A well-dressed man arrived at Truffles about one o'clock in the afternoon. Beaming at the maître d', the gentleman said he had heard a lot about the restaurant and was eager to enjoy a meal.

After being seated, he listened attentively to the sommelier's wine suggestions and tasted several glasses before ordering a four-course meal. He complimented the waiter on the fine service, said nice things about the chef's exquisite creations, and chatted with the maître d' about the décor. He ate slowly and with great relish as a waiter continually replenished his wine glass.

"Dessert is a must after such a great meal," he announced, "but let us not forget the cheese selection."

After the cheese course, he ordered fresh berries and washed them down with a glass of Taylor Port. That was followed by a good cigar and a glass of Louis XIII cognac. He had never before ordered such an expensive cognac, he said, but today was a good day.

At four o'clock he finished the last of the cognac, doused his cigar, and asked to speak to the manager. The on-duty manager hurried over and the well-dressed diner was full of compliments about the hotel, the food, and the service. "I have one last favor to ask," the guest said.

"Certainly," the manager replied. "What can we do for you?"

"Would you please call the police and have me arrested? I have no money. I promise not to create a scene. I expect you to lay charges."

The manager was only too happy to honor the guest's request.

B ad behavior at the hotel wasn't always restricted to guests. Hotel employees could also provide their own unique set of problems.

Human resource departments become very important in a hotel's operation along with the department heads when it comes to proper screening to hire the right staff. But despite best efforts, curious things can happen.

A lunch guest asked us to store some equipment for him that included an $800 camera. When he came to pick it up, the camera had disappeared. The insurance would not cover it. The banquet manager and I were blamed for the loss and ended up buying the guest a new camera.

Police were called to investigate, but they found nothing. Two years later, a camera was brought into a repair shop. The clerk checked the serial number against a list of stolen cameras and sure enough, this proved to be the camera stolen from us. Questioned by police, the owner claimed he bought it in a bar. The guy turned out to be one of our employees. A records check showed he had been working the day the camera disappeared. Obviously the employee had taken the camera, but we couldn't prove anything. Ironically, not only was he a nice guy, but he even followed me to the next hotel and used my name as a reference.

Unfortunately, human resources did not check with me before they hired him. One day I rounded the corner and there he was, big smile on his face, shaking my hand, thanking me for the opportunity to work together again.

I tried to smile back. It didn't quite work.

In the hotel business, theft is the problem that never goes away. From waiters overcharging guests and staff helping themselves to expensive food and drink, to guests who feel they paid for it so they might as well take it, the thievery never ends. It's not just soap and shampoos that get lifted. Everything from bathrobes to pillows and even drapes disappear with shocking regularity.

An antique clock was stolen. A shower curtain was removed, along with the curtain rod. A stainless steel convection oven that filled a wall was swiped off our loading dock. Guests backed a van up to the hotel and filled it full of room furniture.

When I allowed an old friend having financial problems to stay at the hotel for a month, I discovered that he had packed up over 100 knives, forks, and spoons that he had swiped. I confronted him and we agreed that it would be best to leave the silverware behind. When I worked in Berlin, all the turkeys for the U.S. Consulate General's Christmas party were stolen.

Most amazing of all, a colleague in the business told me that recently a departing guest stole his dog.

Curiously, guest thieves often express remorse for their crimes. I received a surprising number of apologetic letters accompanied by payment for stolen items. The best letter I ever got arrived on corporate stationary, accompanied by a corporate check for over $1,000 payment for a stolen painting. Of course, the thief got the corporation to pay. More theft.

The worst incident of employee wrong-doing I encountered revolved around a case we were never able to solve, involving a bedeviling, potentially catastrophic, series of fires.

It started with a lampshade on fire, quickly detected and extinguished. The next thing, there were four fires in as many days.

Then nothing.

One week later, more fires were set. Lampshades burned in hallways, tablecloths burst into flames in empty function rooms. Closed circuit TV cameras were not common at the time so we relied on our own security, the staff, and on our limited technical systems.

We had meetings with the fire department and police. Everyone concluded that an arsonist was at work, and that he or she was one of the hotel staff. We organized a war room where we listed the fires by day, time, and location. Soon a pattern emerged: the fires were usually set Thursdays, Fridays, Saturdays, and, occasionally, Sundays. They mainly occurred after 4 p.m. and never later than 11 p.m.

All staff members working on these days were checked out against their length of service, prior incidents, pending grievances, etc. The police also ran a check of criminal records. To my surprise, we had people working for us who had been convicted of murder, rape, prostitution, and armed robbery. After those revelations came to light, it became difficult to look at certain staff members the same way again.

Despite the array of criminal convictions represented, no one had been convicted of arson. The fires continued in the hotel as the list of staff members under suspicion slowly shrank. Eventually, the number of suspects was reduced to six males: five part-time banquet waiters and our banquet manager.

By now the number of fires had grown to astronomical proportions. In one six-week period up to Valentine's Day, we had 66 fires, everything from a burning table skirt to a linen cart.

A waitress spotted someone leaving an empty ballroom just after a linen cart burst into flame. The man the waitress saw was one of our suspects. The employee was interrogated by detectives. He had been arrested for being in possession of stolen hockey tickets but never charged.

He did admit to socializing with the other men under suspicion, but we could get nothing else out of him. The following day we dismissed the six suspects in the case and immediately the fires stopped. A short time later at the Hilton Hotel, a man was severely burned by a flash fire. Interestingly, one of the dismissed employees was working there at the time, but once again nothing could be proven.

All the police could ever come up with was a wild notion that because our suspects knew each other socially, they might have had a falling out among themselves, and somehow decided to set the fires.

I shook my head in disbelief when I heard this. But then again it made as much sense as anything I encountered in this business.

Chapter Eleven

I have wonderful memories of the Hyatt Regency. The hotel I knew and helped get started is no more. It is now the Four Seasons Hotel of Toronto and quite different than it was when I was there. Original touches remain here and there, evoking many memories. But there was no doubt that as time went on things changed, and not for the better as far as I was concerned.

My boss, Frans Schutzman, was transferred to the new UN Hyatt New York. A new general manager, Dan McKinnon, arrived from England. Our resident manager, Manfred Gerling, moved on and June White, the general manager's secretary, also left (although she followed me to my next job). Several others I worked with were transferred to faraway places where Hyatt was opening new hotels.

The hotel itself was tired and in need of major renovation. After five successful years, the high traffic flow had taken its toll. In 1977 Hyatt lost the management contract to the Four Seasons Hotels.

A group of colleagues and myself had started the Food and Beverage Managers Association. One of the founding members, John Williams, food and beverage director at the Four Seasons

Sheraton Hotel, the vast 1,400-room convention hotel directly across from Toronto's City Hall, offered me a job as director of catering. It meant a huge increase in salary, almost doubling what I was earning.

In April 1975, I left the Hyatt and made my way over to the Sheraton. The excitement and challenge of running a huge convention facility, coupled with the salary increase, was irresistible. With the Hyatt Regency falling behind the times, and no improvement in sight, it was time to leave.

By now, we had been in Canada over a decade. Our son Stephan was ten and his brother Ralph just 14 months behind him. Helga and I had moved the kids from the one-bedroom flat where we started our new life in Canada, into a brand new two-bedroom apartment in Don Mills. Our first car, a 1966 bare-bones Rambler (total cost: $2,242), had been replaced by a yellow Volvo, a real lemon. From the lemon I had graduated to an American Motors station wagon and from there to a shiny Cadillac Seville. *That* was more like it.

Ralph and Stephan growing up.

I missed so much of the boys' growing up. Fortunately, the boys had Helga as mother and part-time father. At one point I was working such long hours people in our neighborhood thought she was a divorcee or widow. I left early in the morning for work and returned late at night.

The first day I arrived at the Four Seasons Sheraton, I could not find the elevator to my new office. The place was that vast. When I eventually reached the office, I was greeted by the man I was replacing, Lou Wizemann. He was moving back to the U.S. with the company. Lou had done an amazing job reorganizing the huge catering office and banquet facility, yet the hotel continued to suffer from the same problems it had when it opened in 1972, including an image as a "bad" American corporate citizen. Partly this was due to the differing political views of Chile.

Canada had friendly relations with Chile's socialist government led by the democratically elected president, Salvador Allende. However, ITT, the conglomerate that owned Sheraton, notoriously supported the military junta led by Augusto Pinochet when it overthrew Allende's government in 1973 (Allende himself committed suicide). The news of ITT's involvement had been trumpeted in black headlines around the world just as the Toronto hotel opened.

The hotel's attempts to improve its image were met with nothing but criticism. A plan to bring chefs from all over the world to introduce an array of international cuisine was perceived as an American hotel out to teach Canadians how to eat with a knife and fork. Every negative incident received headlines, from a ceiling tile in a ballroom that fell prior to the Queen's arrival, to people killing themselves falling off the hotel's steep escalators.

A singles party promoted as the largest such event ever held in Toronto was so over-promoted and badly managed that 25,000 people showed up blocking major arteries in the downtown core. That embarrassing fumble cost the hotel its liquor license for two weeks, not to mention the reassignment of two general managers.

With these events filling local papers, upper management did not last long. Finally, Kai Herbranson, a long time Sheraton vice president in Hawaii, was sent to take charge of the Toronto operation.

He restructured the management team and brought me on board, hoping that my good reputation in the city would add more warmth and character to the operation. The difficulties running a major hotel were compounded by the fact that the Sheraton was next door to Toronto City Hall. A labyrinth of interconnecting passageways brought thousands of visitors—passersby looking for a washroom, criminals in search of something to steal, vagrants looking for a place to sleep. At one time the lower floor washrooms were a popular rendezvous for gay men.

A smart, strong management team is essential to properly oversee a large organization. Traditionally, hotels are divided into the Back of the House and Front of the House. The Front of the House is that part of the hotel where customers can access bars, restaurants, and the lobby, while the Back is where housekeeping, engineering, kitchens and other departments are handled.

The general manager usually oversees the comptroller as well as security, human resources, IT, retail management, and sales and marketing. Each operation may have its own organization chart, particularly in chain hotels where regional management looks after special projects such as renovation and construction or public relations and marketing.

When I got there, the Four Seasons Sheraton's slogan was "A city in itself." It certainly was that. The hotel complex sat on four acres of land. It featured a 25-foot-tall waterfall in its lobby, and a 20,000-square-foot ballroom that could seat 2,000 for dinner.

A state-of-the art exhibit hall was big enough for four tractor-trailer trucks to back into it at the same time. There were 68 retail shops, 11 bars and restaurants, two cinemas, a rooftop lounge, and, for good measure, a prestigious men's fitness club, the Cambridge.

The hotel was so large that to expedite room service breakfast orders, an elevator was set up with tea, coffee, juices, danishes, and muffins. We called it the Flying Breakfast. Five minutes after customers placed an order, they were sipping coffee and munching a muffin.

The hotel was well designed for high traffic volumes. We could handle up to 10,000 guests checking in for a convention. That many breast-feeding mothers showed up as part of La Leche League International. Everywhere you looked, a mother was breast-feeding her baby, not to mention a lot of men changing diapers. Imagine the diaper disposal at the end of the day. Somehow we managed it.

A city within itself, indeed.

My first major challenge was to keep that slogan alive, not an easy task considering what happened shortly after my arrival.

We were to be the headquarters hotel for a United Nations Congress on Crime. Arrangements had been made for the arrival of thousands of delegates. Then Yasser Arafat, at the time leader of the Palestine Liberation Organization (PLO), announced he would attend.

Depending on how you viewed him, Arafat could be seen either as terrorist or statesman. Whatever he was, he was a lightning rod for anger and controversy, so much so that eventually the UN cancelled the convention barely two months before it was supposed to get under way.

That left the hotel in a fine fix. We and the city had been gearing up for a month-long conference. Now it had evaporated. An emergency meeting was convened to decide what to do next.

I suggested we dramatize the tremendous economic losses by showing the hotel's vast, empty ballroom, emphasizing the number of job losses. Our advertising agency loved the idea. CTV reporter Glenn Cochrane promised to do a story built around me starting in my new position only to see the biggest convention of my life disappear overnight.

In addition, an ad soon appeared showing me sitting at a table in a corner of a deserted ballroom full of empty tables. Above our slogan, "It's a city in itself," a hand-written "empty" was added. The caption beneath the ad read: "Why is this man not smiling? He just kissed one million dollars goodbye!"

The publicity introduced me in my new position while pointing out that we had some great deals in place thanks to the cancellation of the UN conference. It received so much attention that business for the hotel and Toronto tourism actually increased. It reminded me again of the ripple effect a convention has on the entire city, not just at the hotel.

A convention draws many people and therefore produces more work for everyone from airport employees and duty-free stores to porters, taxi drivers, and hotel employees. Energy use increases when there is a convention in town; even the number of movies rented goes up. When the conventions don't come, the reverse is true—everyone suffers.

The newspaper ad says it all.

Chapter Twelve

Gradually, I helped improve the Sheraton Hotel's rather shaky local image. I came up with the idea of fishing weekends, stocking the 25-foot waterfall with 2,000 dinner-sized Rainbow trout. I bought 50 fishing rods, set up a blackboard with a menu listing the kinds of bait available, and issued "fishing licenses." Fishing season at the Sheraton kicked off with a press conference featuring a group of children from Variety Village, many of them about to have their first fishing experience. Each hotel guest could catch up to six trout, and we would prepare them to their liking in one of our restaurants at no charge.

We got involved with Newfoundland's fisheries minister and Eastern Provincial Airlines for a seafood promotion, highlighted by the arrival via air of 800 fresh East Coast lobsters. As soon as they got to the hotel, we excitedly opened them, anticipating the fine fresh lobster meat we were all about to enjoy.

It was not to be. Eight hundred lobsters had all gone bad. Precooked and still warm, the lobsters had been stuffed into plastic bags and shipped. Not good for lobsters, we discovered.

Hurriedly the East Coast lobsters were replaced by local crustaceans. Even so, the promotion was a huge hit.

A United Way rock concert, arranged by CHUM FM, featuring three different bands, was almost too successful. When the doors opened, 2,500 kids stampeded for the best seats before the bands were ready to go on. It was December so I suggested Santa make an appearance as a way of keeping things going until the first band arrived on stage.

Big mistake.

The crowd howled its displeasure. They were too old to believe in Santa. Undaunted, Santa lurched on stage, blinded by the spotlight, tripping over the cables and the kids sitting on the floor. The kids started screaming that there is no Santa Claus and to prove it, they rushed the stage, pulled Santa's wig and beard off, tore his jacket open, and yanked away the pillows employed to give him heft, leaving a skinny Irish lad with red hair shaking in his boot— the crowd having ripped the other one off.

The mob then proceeded to tear the place apart, using the edges of pop cans to rip open seat cushions, throwing the foam at one another. The police decided discretion was the better part of valor and let them go at it. Three hundred chairs were destroyed. The host, CHUM FM's morning man Roger Ashby, could only watch in stunned silence. We still talk about it, shaking our heads.

We had much better luck with baseball. In fact, baseball helped put the hotel on the map both locally and internationally. For that I have to thank Paul Godfrey. When I first met him, Paul had just become chairman of Metro Toronto. We met following a luncheon for NATO generals, of all things. Newly arrived in town, the generals attended a reception in their honor only to discover they had to pay for their drinks. As Metro Chairman, Paul was the host. He arrived late, saw the problem, and immediately tried to pay for the generals' drinks. Unfortunately, no one recognized the youthful-looking Paul or believed he was one of the most powerful men in city government. They would not allow him to charge the drinks.

When I heard what happened, I met with Paul and his assistant, Ray Biggart, who I knew from the Walker House days. I assured

Blue Jays memories.

them that whenever there was a Metro function, I would be there. That was the beginning of a long friendship with both men.

Paul, as Metro Chairman, was a driving force in bringing Blue Jays baseball to town, along with Paul Beeston and Howie Starkman. He no sooner got the Jays moved into what was then the SkyDome (now the Rogers Centre) than he decided to go after the annual Major League Baseball convention, normally held early in December.

Few believed Paul could persuade the owners. But then everyone underestimated Paul. He arrived in Hawaii and went to work. The next thing, I got a call from him. Somehow, he'd convinced the owners to hold the convention in snow-swept Toronto in December. We virtually booked the massive convention over the phone. Six hundred club owners, players, financial gurus of the industry and their legal teams, as well as 300 sports media people from around the world were all headed for Toronto. Everyone would be talking about the Sheraton Centre, everyone eating and drinking—a very good piece of business, particularly since December is normally a slow month for conventions.

If Paul is a most enterprising individual, his multi-tasking wife Gina is right behind him. Besides raising three children, she is an accomplished artist and painter who also founded the Herbie Fund charity, raising millions for special surgical care for children. Later, she became a Citizenship Court judge.

Unions were a large part of our convention business, although they were not always the easiest customers to deal with. When we hosted the annual Ontario Federation of Labor convention, one of the 1,500 delegates noticed we were using Stevenson Linens, a U.S. firm that employed non-union workers. The U.S. union had tried for years to organize them to no avail. The little labels in the corners of the tablecloth clearly stated the manufacturer.

Angrily, the delegate yanked the cloth off the table. Others started doing the same. Soon hundreds of union delegates were piling 400 tablecloths into a corner. They demanded management's assurance that all the tablecloths would be destroyed, otherwise, they would never come back to the hotel. One radical character even threatened to set the linen pile on fire.

We quickly got a dozen employees to remove the tablecloths. We then held an emergency meeting with union brass. They were apologetic but couldn't guarantee it wouldn't happen again, even though they knew we could never order so much linen on such short notice.

Fortunately, we had plenty of tablecloths from the same manufacturer but in different colors. We cut the brand tags off each tablecloth and then went about resetting the room. If the delegates guessed what we had done, they thankfully never said anything, and left the tablecloths alone.

We nearly had another riot starring 1,000 delegates from the International Rubber Workers Union. The delegates, as was usually the case, were pre-charged for meals. The hotel then requires a guaranteed number of meals in order to schedule staff, create menus, and purchase food. Often the organizers count on delegates not showing up for meals and lowball the numbers they give us in hopes of pocketing the difference.

When delegates began arriving for the annual dinner, it soon became apparent there were a lot more diners than the organizer had told us. What's more, the organizer was insisting that any guest without a ticket would not be served. Well, try telling a burly union man he can't have the roast beef he already paid for simply because he doesn't have a lousy ticket. Chaos ensued. There simply were not enough seats.

Soon we had 150 people milling angrily on the dance floor. The head table was refusing to seat itself. The situation grew more intense by the minute. Red-faced guests confronted seated diners waving tickets in their faces. Fistfights were about to break out.

The chef and I huddled together. We decided we would have to serve more meals, get more tables into the ballroom, and reassign staff. The longer the guests waited the angrier everyone became. Finally, the head table more or less crept into the room and once the unseated guests saw that, they swarmed them. In the midst of the chaos, the organizer, the guy who had gotten us into this mess, faked a heart attack. We carried him out of the hall through the milling, pushing throng and hid him in the beverage manager's office.

I went back and confronted the union president who I realized was pretty drunk. We could serve 100 more guests but the rest had to go either to our dining room or to a restaurant across the street. The president stepped before the microphone, trying to bring order. No one paid any attention. I asked him if I might try. Go ahead, he said.

I took the microphone and announced that I was serving everyone a free drink. Immediately, silence descended in the room. All eyes were on me. The free drinks, I continued, would be served in the lobby to everyone who would eat dinner somewhere else and return later for the entertainment.

A murmur of approval went up. People began to make their way to the lobby, understanding the evening otherwise would be spoiled. The staff rolled in 10 more tables and served the very well-done roast beef, while I attended to the rest of the guests. I felt sorry for these people. They had traveled from small communities— hard-working men and women who looked forward to a few days

Getting into gear for Christmas; Sheraton's A Team.

in the big city. I escorted our overflow guests to the Redwoods Restaurant and then directed others across the street.

Crisis averted. More or less.

The Sheraton Centre is very much a convention hotel. The business was then, and is now, seasonal. January is mostly dead. Then in mid-February business begins to pick up into the busy months of April through to the end of June. Summer slows again, and then it usually becomes very busy from September through November. December convention business, perhaps not surprisingly, is non-existent once you are in the second week. Banquets keep a hotel going during the holidays.

At the Sheraton we could easily push out 5,000 dinners from the banquet kitchen alone, speeding toward 20 different function rooms. With dozens of heated trucks on wheels lined up to deliver food, the atmosphere was often chaotic. It took a chef with a cool head to keep everything moving smoothly.

Not only was it the time of year for banquets, but also for

Santa Claus. He became *de rigeur* at the holiday season. Preparing 5,000 meals was easy compared to the difficulties with our various Santas.

It was my bad luck to hire and supervise the sometimes not so-jolly old fellow. I made sure he received a Sheraton name tag— "Santa C"—a pager, as well as a daily list of events. I instructed him where and when to go, touring our shops, bars, and restaurants. He was also available for banquet functions. As long as I kept him to a schedule, everything worked well.

In the evening, however, Santa was left to his own devices. That's when trouble started.

Once Santa drunkenly stumbled through the hotel calling out in a slurred voice, so much of an embarrassment we had to let him go before Christmas. Another St. Nick was no saint at all but something of a ladies man. Women did not seem to mind his advances, but when we twice caught him in the women's washroom, we had to let him go. He insisted the women lured him in there.

Year after year there were problems. During one holiday season, we used Santa in our newly-opened indoor pool's giant hot tub. Following my suggestion, the *Toronto Sun* published a front page photo of Santa sitting in the tub, his beard blown dry by an attractive young lady in a bikini. Outraged parents bombarded the *Sun* and our switchboard with complaints, not because Santa posed with a bikini-clad beauty, but for the stupidity of using an electric blow dryer in a hot tub. They were right, of course.

My head ached.

The stuff that goes on inside a hotel. Even now it makes me shake my head in amazement. Couples would stop the elevators to have sex between floors. Pranksters put furniture in the elevators. We dealt with streakers and pie throwers. Married couples broke up marriages, loudly, in the middle of the dining room.

The hotel's proximity to both City Hall and the Provincial Court building provided unique experiences. A would-be groom appeared in the lobby desperately looking for his missing best man. No sign of him. The groom looked me up and down, and the next thing I knew I was across the street standing in as best man for a couple I had never met before and have not seen since. I was delighted to be of service.

A convention speaker refused to go on until we found his daughter's teddy bear, taken away by mistake when maids changed the beds. We managed to find it among dirty linen from 1,500 rooms in time for his speech.

Early one morning the chairman of a large corporation called, loudly complaining that we had served his underage son liquor and kept him in the hotel until 3 a.m. I had no idea what he was talking about, but before I could ask any questions, he hung up. A dinner was about to be held in the chairman's honor for 1,800 guests. This was a valuable client. I had to quickly get to the bottom of what happened.

It turned out his son and a friend, after being turned away several times at the bar, had met a couple of flight attendants on the elevator. Being underage, they could not take the attendants into the hotel bars, so they convinced the night manager they were checking on the hospitality suite in advance of the chairman's dinner. Bribing the room service manager to let them buy a bottle of Mumms Champagne, they borrowed a waiter's uniform and arrived at the ladies' room with four glasses and the champagne mounted on a silver tray.

The women were so delighted, they invited the young men to stay the night. The next day, however, the teenager's mother was furious that her son had been out all night in a hotel suite, drinking. As it turned out, the chairman himself was not nearly as angry as he first seemed. If anything, dad was rather proud of his son.

Young people and alcohol and hotels are not usually a good combination. That was never more evident than at spring graduation time. The celebrations were always a problem. We had a strict policy about hosting school proms. We required a signed statement from the principal promising that school authorities and off-duty police officers would be present to ensure no liquor or drugs were brought in. If there was trouble, it usually came when I disregarded those policies—like the time the teenage daughter of a well-known client begged me to let her have a suite for her graduation night. Every other room in town was booked. I was her last resort. I gave in and got her a room.

About two thirty the next morning, the duty staff received several noise complaints. It sounded as though a young woman was being abused in one of the suites. Security phoned the room. No reply. They went up to the room, and as they came along the corridor, they could hear a woman screaming. Security quickly opened the door with a master key. Inside, they found the client's teenage daughter engaged in sex with three men.

More screaming ensued, this time at the security people. It ended with the three guys being evicted in the middle of the night. The young lady must have departed shortly thereafter. The next morning, I had just enough time to read the report of these events, before the girl's irate mother called, upset that her daughter had been thrown out of the hotel at three in the morning. Not surprisingly, she described a totally different scenario than the one I had in front of me.

Sometimes you expect the worst and then are pleasantly surprised. Approached by a client involved with a Catholic Church program that attempted to give young people convicted of minor offences a second chance, I agreed to participate.

Twelve minor offenders showed up to work at the hotel. I warned that if one person among them broke the rules, then everyone suffered and the program would be terminated immediately.

We had no problems at all. If anything, we received compliments on the performance of the young people. Later, I got a letter from the 12, not only thanking us for the things they had learned, but also for giving them a chance, and most importantly, for trusting them.

Not hard at all as it turned out.

It always amazed me what could be accommodated at the Sheraton. Buses could drive up our loading ramp into the hotel. For a convention of funeral directors, fleets of hearses and trucks full of coffins and embalming tables were brought in. A whole garden setting was erected for a landscape convention, including benches, waterfalls, and 20-foot-tall trees.

When Toyota wanted to introduce a new model at the hotel, a custom-built stage, 80 feet long, was constructed with multiple screens, hydraulic lectern, elevator platforms, a fog machine, and a turntable with a real car on it.

We hosted a Tupperware-type convention and the theme had something to do with a bear. Let's rent a bear, I said. I should have kept my mouth shut.

In fact, we found a brown bear, nine feet tall. Brought up on the stage by his trainer, our guest bear did a few tricks and then exited to great applause. As the trainer led the bear down the rear loading ramp to his trailer, the glass recycling bin came to life, making an awful screeching sound. Spooked, the bear swung around, dashing like mad back into the hotel, dragging its screaming trainer behind him.

I was on my way to the ballroom when a bear raced past. No, I thought. That couldn't be a bear. I turned and saw to my horror that a bear was indeed loose in the hotel. Eventually, the trainer calmed the animal and coaxed him back to his trailer. I don't think he had any treats that night.

We never had a lot of luck with animals. Since the hotel overflowed with children during the summer, I suggested a campaign called "Sheraton Loves Kids," eventually copied by other Sheraton hotels. We organized a daily draw in the lobby with prizes, brought in players from the Blue Jays and Argonauts, as well as animals from the Toronto Zoo.

Surprising the things you learn in the hotel business. For instance, during this time I learned camels do not like to walk backwards. Who knew?

Because they don't, the handlers had a difficult time getting our visiting camel out of the trailer. The beast became ever more nervous when it stepped onto the lobby's terrazzo flooring. The handler tried to calm him down but you could see stomach muscles anxiously heaving, not a good sign in a camel.

All of a sudden, the camel emitted a gigantic fart followed by a flood of diarrhea spraying across the lobby, hitting a dozen children who did not realize what had happened until they wiped their faces. And the smell. Camel shit stinks to high heaven.

Another hard lesson learned.

An evening to remember: John Williams, Bill Dinwoodie, me, Steve Saravanja, and chef Hans Stuerzenbecher.

Chapter Thirteen

By the time I got to the Sheraton, the famous were beginning to flock there—everyone from movie stars and the Queen Mother to Israeli Prime Minister Menachem Begin. I remember Begin's visit particularly well. As I stood there watching the prime minister speak, I came to the realization that directly behind him what was supposed to be an Israeli flag was in fact an upside down Quebec flag. A desperate-but-inventive staff member, short a flag, had decided the colors were close enough. Somehow, the banquet manager and I managed to switch flags in front of the prime minister and 1,800 guests. Nobody was the wiser.

Israeli Prime Minister Menachem Begin proposes a toast—after we got the flag right.

At least I don't think they were.

The Queen Mother, with her beautiful smile, reminded me of my mother. She was born in 1900, my mother in 1899. They also were the same height. When they met, my 82-year-old mother curtsied.

They could have been sisters, I thought. I'm only sorry I never got a picture of the two of them together.

When the Queen Mother attended a luncheon at the Sheraton Centre, everyone of course came dressed to the hilt. Ladies wore huge hats, while some of the men were in morning frocks. Everything seemed to go swimmingly. But then executive chef Leo Schuster got a bit carried away with his *pièce de résistance*, a finely diced medley of herbs and artichoke bottoms topped with a lamb chop the size of a ham hock wrapped in a filo pastry. The lamb chop towered over the plate.

Serving it, we heard many appreciative "Oohs" and "Aahs." From everyone but the Queen Mother.

She took an elegantly Royal look at her huge lamb chop and did not touch it. When discreet inquires were made wondering if she might prefer something else, she politely declined. On her way back to the suite, our manager, David Hamilton, a British citizen, asked her if she enjoyed her luncheon.

The Queen Mother paused before she said of the lamb chop, "It looked like a citadel. I did not know how to tackle it." She then asked for a glass of sherry before retiring for her afternoon nap.

To Hans Gerhardt
With best wishes.
Ronald Reagan

President Ronald Reagan

A popular luncheon series, Universal Speakers, also drew many famous people over the years, including U.S. presidents Ronald Reagan and Gerald Ford, German chancellor Helmut Schmidt, CBS news anchor Walter Cronkite, diplomat Henry Kissinger, former secretary of state Alexander Haig, economic presidential advisor and author Arthur Schlesinger Jr., columnist George Will.

Media baron Conrad Black, along with his brother Montague, often presided as did CTV anchor

Lloyd Robertson. The luncheons provided opportunities for both Black brothers to network, as they did for the owners of Universal Speakers, Harry Littler and Brian Seater.

I always admired the Blacks for the eloquence they brought to thanking their guests. They employed an often mesmerizing vocabulary, throwing out words unknown to many in the audience. They looked like royalty in both the manner they walked and the way they spoke, particularly Conrad Black. Every word out of his mouth seemed to be carefully chosen. They always acknowledged me with a nod—friendly, but not too friendly.

Bringing celebrities to the hotel was also a great feather in our caps since the luncheons always received extensive media coverage and drew Canada's business elite to the hotel. I usually managed to get myself into the thick of things. Ronald Reagan appeared the same year he became president. He gave me one of his pens with his name on it. Arthur Schlesinger detected my German accent and we discovered that he went to school in the late 1930s just opposite where I lived in Berlin's Wilmersdorfer Strasse. We chatted in German for quiet a while.

By contrast, Henry Kissinger, who was German, and whom I met on three occasions, never said a word in our native language. Author George Plimpton, in addition to writing the bestselling *Paper Lion*, was also known for his love of fireworks and for being simply delightful. The night before his speech, Helga and I had dinner with him. Dazzling.

Actor Charlton Heston, on tour for his book *My Journals*, rushed to the hotel from the airport to drop off his bags so he could get to a live television interview. He was looking forward to a very rare steak and a glass of red wine. "How about a half a bottle of 1961 Château Margaux Grand Cru?" he asked.

The steak and the wine would be waiting when he got back, I promised. Meanwhile, boxes of books arrived in his suite so he could pre-sign for the next day's event. When he arrived back, I told him our chef would cook the steak in his suite to ensure it was

With Charlton Heston.

rare. However, we did not have his favorite wine by the half bottle. A full bottle of Château Margaux would cost $475. Heston asked if I had eaten dinner, and when I said I hadn't, he invited me to join him. How could I say no to the man who played Moses and Ben-Hur?

"In that case, let's have the full bottle," he said.

We had a delightful dinner during which he talked about how he developed his book, recounted tales of his world travels, and described the great hotels he had stayed in. He even gave me his home address in Los Angeles and insisted I call him when I was in town. When we finished eating, I offered to help him sign his books. I opened the covers so that he could quickly sign and then replaced the books in the boxes.

We worked like a team. Once in a while he paused, had a sip of wine, and then went back to work. Soon we discovered the bottle was empty. "Let's have another, shall we?" Heston said.

And we did.

When my pager went off, I told him it was most likely my wife

Helga wondering where I was. He insisted on talking to her.

"Hi, this is Chuck," he said. "Chuck Heston. I am the one to blame for keeping your husband up this late."

Helga had heard lots of excuses over the years. She was not buying into this one. Heston insisted she drop by the suite. When she arrived an hour later, he opened the door to greet her. Helga was speechless.

The three of us dined together the next night, as well. More Château Margaux was consumed. Possibly much more. The bill for Charlton Heston's wine? Two thousand dollars. The book publicist nearly had a heart attack. I arranged for a generous discount to ease her pain.

Not all celebrities who visited the Sheraton were as trouble-free as Charlton Heston. The British pop singer Petula Clark, best known for the 1960s hit, "Downtown," arrived to perform with a 12-piece band following a gala convention dinner for IBM.

She and her husband, Claude Wolff, insisted they had to have a concert grand piano for the performance. That proved to be difficult to acquire for a single performance. Paul Hahn, who tuned the eight pianos in the hotel, had a concert grand in his private collection and agreed to let us have it for Petula Clark's performance.

The piano was beautiful and it looked great on the stage. However, Wolff insisted we remove the lid. I had assured Paul Hahn that no one would touch his grand piano other than to play it. Now, here was the star's husband demanding that the lid be removed.

I told Clark's people that I would have to get permission from the owner. As soon as I walked away, someone got a screwdriver and removed the lid.

That night I watched the show and saw that the lid was off the piano. I gulped and crossed my fingers, praying that everything would be all right. First thing next morning, I got a call from our director of convention services, Fred Kippert. He asked me to come down and look at something. The grand piano lid lay on the floor of the now-empty ballroom. A forklift truck, in the process of moving out equipment, had run over it, splitting the lid in half.

I almost broke into tears. This beautiful piano was destroyed. The convener, while upset, assured me he would look after the costs of the repairs. Paul Hahn hurried over to the hotel. He guessed something was wrong but not this. Angry and upset, he immediately canceled his contract with the hotel and announced that he would sue. We eventually settled out of court. Sadly, it was not enough to mend our long-standing friendship. We never did business again.

A friend, Bill Bannon, who channeled a lot of business my way, got me involved with Micheal Lee Aday, better known as Meat Loaf. The burly rock singer's career had just taken off thanks to his album, *Bat Out of Hell* (it would go on to sell over 40 million copies).

To celebrate its success, his record company was flying in 250 media from the U.S. and Canada for an extravaganza telecast live on both CTV and CBS. The plan was for Meat Loaf to enter the Dominion ballroom riding a great white horse. He would then dismount to sit on a throne while caftan-clad guests sprawled on pillows underneath a tent in an oasis-like setting with palm trees, hookahs, Middle-Eastern musicians, harem girls, and waiters dressed as eunuchs. Oh, yes. An eagle, a zebra, a lion, and a camel would also be present.

The first time I heard about all this, I had reservations, but no one on the hotel's executive committee paid any attention—until the day before it was to happen. That's when George Mallon, our area comptroller, who had never heard of Meat Loaf, like most of us, summoned me to vice president Kai Herbranson's office. They wanted me to go over the plan again, particularly the part about the lion, the camel, the zebra, and eagle, not to mention this unheard of rock star who would be riding a white horse.

When I finished, Mallon asked me if I was all right. "Can you imagine," he said, "if the horse and the lion don't get along and this hot rock star is thrown off? Can you imagine the law suit? The publicity?"

He became almost hysterical. The event had to be cancelled. It could not take place. We had to call head office and ask our lawyer Larry Iron for legal advice. I was shocked. What had Mallon been thinking? I'd talked about all this for the past three weeks.

George apparently thought I was kidding. Well, I was not. Here we were one day before the event. The organizer had spent thousands on the pre-planning. We had no choice but to go forward, armed with a release relieving the hotel of any responsibility, and a $2 million dollar insurance policy.

It's a good thing we took those precautions. Meat Loaf arrived having celebrated a bit too much in advance. Four people were required to lift him onto the horse and then guide him into the ballroom, two leading the horse and two on either side holding him up. Fortunately, the horse remained calm as we tried and failed several times before finally lifting Meat Loaf into the saddle.

Somehow it all worked. The animals all behaved even if the humans didn't.

Occasionally, celebrities became friends. Legendary Canadian actor Al Waxman and his wife Sara had become close, although there was an occasion when our friendship was sorely tested.

Old friends Al and Sara Waxman.

Best known in Canada as CBC-TV's *King of Kensington*, Al had gone on to international fame co-starring in the long-running CBS crime series, *Cagney & Lacey*. Sara was a well-known Toronto writer and food critic. Al was commuting back and forth between Los Angeles and Toronto, but he always made time to be at charity events such as the annual Cancer Fashion Show fundraiser

Al was a stickler about time. Sara agreed to leave the fundraiser no later than 1:45 p.m. When the show was delayed, she suggested Al get their coats and bring the car around, which he did. By 2 p.m., Al was still standing outside while Sara remained inside with 2,000 people watching the show.

Al kept impatiently looking at his watch. It was getting really late and he needed her for their next appointment. That's when I made the mistake of saying, "Wouldn't it be fun to send one of the police officers to get your wife?"

Al looked at me. His eyes lit up. "Yeah," he said. "Let's do it."

An officer assigned to the event eagerly agreed to go along with our scheme. We pointed to the table where Sara was sitting, the blond lady in a beige dress.

Off he went. Al and I stood peeking through the door like two little boys. We watched while the policeman walked straight to the wrong table. We watched him being directed to another wrong table. Then he got the wrong person. Then another table where Sara wasn't sitting and another woman who wasn't Sara.

All of a sudden this did not seem funny any more.

By now the room was buzzing. A cop roamed the room, confronting various women, on the hunt for a suspect named Sara Waxman. What had happened? What was wrong?

Al and I broke into a cold sweat. Finally, he found Sara. She reacted with alarm, thinking something had happened to Al. All eyes were on her as she rushed out to be confronted by a sheepish-looking Al. Concern turned to rage. I beat a hasty retreat. Al told me later that my idea had cost him a fur coat and he was still late for his appointment!

Sometimes the joke worked. Gordon Ostlere was known to the world as Richard Gordon, British author of a series of comic doctor novels beginning in 1952 with *Doctor in the House*. The books were international bestsellers spawning movies and a TV series. Dr. Gordon was as funny as his characters and wrote from his own experiences.

When he gave a lecture at the hotel, he told the story of a man whose head leaned to the left side of his shoulder. Meeting him at a cocktail party, Dr. Gordon suggested hypnosis to correct the deformity. It worked. The man's head straightened. To celebrate, the man bought himself and Dr. Gordon a drink.

"Cheers," he said, lifting the glass to his mouth—Dr. Gordon threw a glass of water over his left shoulder—missing his mouth entirely because, well, that's not where his head was any longer. Laughter and applause. Water drenched the wall.

I thanked the doctor for his speech, glaring at the wall. "I'm supposed to give you a beautiful Rosenthal plate showing Toronto's Old City Hall," I said. "But given the damage you've caused here tonight, I'm not going to do it."

I turned and walked off the stage. Dr. Gordon stood there, his mouth open. A moment later, I came back with his plate. Just joking. Relieved laughter spread through the hall. Dr. Gordon accepted the plate with a rueful smile. "That could have been one of my lines," he said.

Chapter Fourteen

An economic turndown in the early 1980s badly hurt the hotel business. We are always selling a time frame that cannot be banked. Once the bed is empty for the night or a chair is not occupied during a meal, that time frame cannot be replaced. Rooms have to be occupied, seats filled, or we are out of business.

I suggested we look at alternative ways to get bodies into rooms and bums into seats. To accomplish this, we established an annual promotional budget of $125,000. My title was changed to director of promotions and catering. With the help of Catherine McAuley, whom I promoted from catering sales manager to become my assistant, we laid out an aggressive creative marketing and sales program with the help of the Sheraton Centre team.

Not all promotions worked quite the way I hoped. The fishing weekends, for example, had their problems. The waterfall was not properly secured, allowing many of the 2,000 rainbow trout to escape into an area inaccessible to the fishing public. Days later, hundreds of the trout were poisoned by a gardener's herbicide spray, killing not only the fish but my promotion. Thousands of gallons of water were replaced, the fish stock replenished. The

Catherine McAuley,
my wonderful assistant.

promotion went on to great success, thanks in part to the terrific media coverage orchestrated by our public relations team headed by Pam Jackson and her assistant, Leanne Sharpe.

The last episode of the hit CBS television comedy series, *M*A*S*H*, inspired me to create a *M*A*S*H* Bash, duplicated by several Sheraton Hotels across the continent. Its success won me a second North American Sheraton President Marketing and Promotions award.

We installed a vintage Jeep in the main lobby to promote the bash. A front page *Sun* photo featured Metro Chairman Paul Godfrey, popular radio host Don Daynard, and his sidekick, Jeremy Brown, who also acted as master of ceremonies along with CBC-TV hostess Barbara McLeod.

The hall was decorated to resemble the set on the TV show, complete with ambulances and military vehicles and camouflage netting strung overhead.

The Sheraton staff recreated the officer's latrine and the directional sign post, set the tables with tin plates and cheap aluminum cutlery. Guests came dressed as the characters on the show. We even had a competition for the guest who looked most like a series character—Klinger won hands down, except our Klinger had a beard.

Towards the end of the evening, I was with Citytv reporter J.D.

Roberts (later John Roberts of CNN), who was doing a story on the event, when I noticed a young guy sleeping on a bench. When I tried to wake him up, I was jumped from behind by his drunken friend yelling at me to mind my own business. I told him who I was. That didn't help. The drunk threatened to punch me out.

When they finally left the bar and headed for a white Cadillac parked in our motor court, we tried to persuade them not to drive. They responded by attempting to run me over. Fortunately, stainless steel bumpers anchored in front of the lobby doors protected me.

Having failed to hit me, one of the passengers yanked out a silver handgun and started waving it around. Tires screeching, the Cadillac sped away. I managed to get the New York license plate number and called the police. Obviously these hard-drinking, Cadillac-driving, gun-waving New Yorkers were not M*A*S*H fans.

Not everything we did was as successful as the M*A*S*H Bash. When workout guru Richard Simmons agreed to do two shows for us, we sent out 50 press releases in an Adidas running shoe with a note that said, "Start your day on the right foot and join the Richard Simmons Show." To get the left shoe, you had attend his press conference. Of course, everyone did, and that produced wide media coverage. Even so, Richard lost money for us.

Still, we kept at it, involving everyone from band leader Count Basie to rocker Ronnie Hawkins in our promotions. We constantly reviewed booking patterns. When we saw business lagging, we created a promotional event. This raised stress levels considerably, but I had a wonderful team—my assistant Catherine, Tim Lilleyman who ran catering, Hans Stuerzenbecher, Ron Merpaw, and Dermot McKeown. Working together, we somehow managed repeatedly to pull the rabbits out of the hats.

With so many conventions coming in from the U.S. and around the world, I hired a researcher to find original Canadian recipes. In 1976, I coined "A Taste of Canada" and trademarked it. As part of

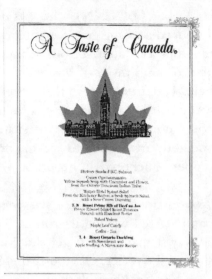

A Taste of Canada.

the "Taste of Canada" project we found a soup that came from the Sixth Nations band called Ogwissimanabo, a delightful concoction of yellow squash, chicken stock, diced cucumbers, a dab of honey, and a sprinkle of parsley.

We served the soup in a small scooped-out squash in the cradle of a rosebud-shaped napkin. It drove executive chef Hans Behrends crazy when it was served to 1,000 people. Every time we featured the soup on the menu, I'd get a call from him that invariably began, "What the f— are you thinking?"

He asked a similar question when we sold handmade chocolate cups filled with a dark and white chocolate mousse laced with Quebec maple syrup. These creations required a large team, but they were always a success, and the "Taste of Canada" events over the years enchanted thousands of visitors.

They were so successful that I coined "Taste of Toronto" after well-known cartoonist Ben Wicks and his wife Doreen approached me to help them raise money for hospital equipment in Third World countries. The idea behind "A Taste of Toronto" was to assign chefs from hotels and restaurants around the city to create samples of their cuisine, for a wider audience.

Ben had written a bestselling book, *No Time to Wave Goodbye*, about his experiences during the war as one of the children sent to Canada to escape the rockets raining down on London, England. I explained that I was born in Peenemünde, the place where the rockets that forever changed Ben's life were designed and built by people who included my father.

Ben and I looked at each other with tears in our eyes. How ironic that two children of war, all these years later, could come together as friends. With his wicked sense of humor, Ben suggested he might introduce me that evening. I demurred. It was not a night for sons of German rocket specialists.

John Ryan, who operated the tour desk and the concierge services at the Sheraton, wanted to establish a dinner theater at the hotel. By coincidence, we were approached by a young entrepreneur-actor-producer, Richard Comar, with the idea of staging something called *Yuppies, the Musical*. Witty and very timely, given the emergence of the yuppie era, the show was a success. John was even more convinced that we had the right concept, and with my encouragement, created a show business division in his burgeoning empire.

That was a mistake, as it turned out. After a couple of years doing various productions, he lost over $100,000 and closed down his show business with a final production aptly titled *What a Way to Go*. John saved the poster from the show and hung it in his boardroom. Whenever he thinks about going back into show business, he closes the door and sits looking at the poster, thinking of me. In fact he still calls me, ruefully, "Mr. Show Biz."

After a few minutes in the boardroom, the show business desire goes away.

Chapter Fifteen

We kept coming up with new and unusual ways to keep the hotel in the spotlight. When Toronto police instituted the RIDE program over the Christmas season to stop drunk driving, we offered local companies a "RIDE an Elevator Home" package for employees attending events at the hotel. Big success.

There was almost nothing we wouldn't try, including dressing a golf cart to look like a locomotive pulling an instant buffet consisting of five food-laden trailers, proceeded by a marching band. Two thousand convention guests loved it.

Another time when the Ontario Government had an election and no liquor could be served until the polls closed, I loaded up a mini 1930s Oldsmobile convertible replica with magnums of Champagne. At eight o'clock sharp, as soon as the polls closed, a band started playing "Happy Days Are Here Again." Banquet manager Steven Saravanja and I, dressed like bootleggers, drove the Olds into the ballroom so that 100 waiters could serve champagne to guests. A huge success.

Frank Fournier used to run promotions for PetroCanada. He called one day to ask if I could talk to one of his associates,

Bill Simpkins. Bill, an avid photographer, had met two guys, Rick Smolan and David Cohen, who were finishing a photo book titled *A Day in the Life of Hawaii*. The idea was to put 100 internationally known photographers into a country and then take pictures over a 24-hour period. They wanted to do their next book on Canada and were looking for potential sponsors. I liked Rick and David immediately and loved their concept. I convinced my bosses to sponsor the project to the tune of $125,000. Rick and David now had a home for their project and were able to quickly line up additional sponsors. The resulting coffee-table book sold 250,000 copies and enabled them to publish similar books on Japan, Russia, and the United States.

Every time I see one of their books, it gives me great satisfaction knowing I helped get them started.

Not every scheme I concocted went off as planned. For the Queen's Jubilee, we displayed fake Crown Jewels, dressed a mannequin as a Beefeater, and for dessert served classic ice cream cake or *bombe glacée*. We topped a seven-foot-high fake cake with a large silver bowl filled with methyl hydrate. As the cake was paraded into the room followed by 200 waiters, a band played and people clapped along.

Alas, the entrance door was wider than the exit door. When the four waiters carrying the cake tilted it so they could go through the exit, the methyl hydrate spilled, setting the cake and the carpet on fire. Fortunately, banquet manager Manuel Vaz quickly extinguished the blaze.

Catering sales manager Bob Overend asked me to donate a prize for the annual Sales and Marketing Association dinner. How about "An Evening to Remember" in the form of a dinner for eight served amid the vastness of a Grand Ballroom seating 2,000 guests?

The winners and their guests were picked up in two limousines and driven right into the ballroom. They were greeted by a hotel executive dressed in tails and escorted to a table in the center of the room beautifully set with candelabras, fine crystal glassware, gold-plated cutlery, show plates, and antique Bergere chairs. A harpist in a flowing white dress sat on an elevated platform among palm trees.

Once the guests were seated, food and beverage director John Williams read the menu from a scroll, first in French and then in English. Each course had its show piece, such as a lobster pyramid or an encrusted soup terrine, the crust ceremoniously carved open by our banquet chef Hans Stuerzenbecher in white tails and a chef's hat.

After serving several entrees, the *pièce de résistance* was wheeled in with great fanfare, revealed beneath the silver dome of a carving wagon—that internationally renowned dish, *chien chaud*, better known in the English-speaking world as the hot dog. It came complete with plastic squirt bottles full of ketchup and mustard. Great laughter and applause ensued. Who, after all, can resist a hot dog?

The story was avidly covered by the local media and abruptly everyone wanted to book their version of dinner in the Grand Ballroom. Next up was a stag party for 40 seated around a hollow-square table decked with fine linen, gold-plated show plates, and our expensive Riedel crystal glassware. Once the limo entered with the surprised groom-to-be, we served a vintage Roederer Cristal Champagne for the toast.

The best man then ceremoniously tossed the expensive champagne flute into the center of the hollow square, followed by 39 more expensive glasses. Stunned, I rushed over to the host, whispering into his ear that he had just broken over $2,000 worth of crystal glasses. He apologized and then ask us to fill glasses again.

As soon as this was done, he announced that indeed they had just broken a lot of very expensive glass. He asked everyone to stand and once again toast the groom. Then he smashed his glass into the hollow. Thirty-nine more glasses followed.

The host saw the look of stricken horror on my face and

smiled. "Just add it to the bill," he said.

And I did.

For the Sheraton North America Food & Beverage conference we were challenged by Stephen Peek, Sheraton's vice president of food and beverages, to really show off. Since it was winter, I suggested a Winter Wonderland with a Canadian theme. A skating rink (actually specially coated plastic tile) was set up in the Dominion Ballroom with an artificial snow-making machine, a dancing bear on skates, children in old-fashioned winter costume and, of course, a snowman. We even had a 12-foot-tall First Nations teepee flown in from Calgary.

Assorted "fire waters" were served from earthen jugs. A huge hip of beef came from Calgary, desserts featured Quebec maple syrup. Newfoundland oysters were shucked by a fisherman in a rowboat. An eight-foot-high igloo with real Inuit carvings made out of Styrofoam by artist-pastry chef Jean-Paul dominated the center of the room. We had to remove an entire glass and steel firewall to get it up to the second floor. For good measure, we arranged for three Siberian Huskies and a sled.

For another convention in conjunction with the Canadian Egg Marketing Board, we urged delegates to "get cracking." In order to help them do that, we brought in stacks of cages containing live chickens. Guests had to walk among the caged chickens in order to enter the ballroom. The chickens welcomed delegates with chicken poop. The odor choked the hall. We brought in big fans to clean out the smell. It lingered for a long time.

Note to idea bank: *do not repeat!*

I found myself unexpectedly thrown into the spotlight during a convention of International Meeting Planners, powerful men and women whose job it is to plan and organize conventions for large and small companies and corporations. Needless to say, hotels bend over backwards to keep these people happy.

Gathering in Toronto at the Sheraton Centre, the meeting

planners at the last moment lost their guest speaker. I was asked to fill in and talk about creative catering. How could I say no?

Introduced as "Franz von Schnitzelhuber," Bavarian music blared as I made my entrance dressed in lederhosen and a Tiroler hat complete with feather. Reaching the podium, I welcomed everyone in a heavy German accent, promising that "Today, we bring an end to the rubber chicken banquet dinner era!"

In a more serious vein, I talked about how to improve convention catering by seeking out interesting local dishes. Toward the end of my speech, I yanked out a rubber chicken and produced a starter pistol. As gasps went up from my audience, I shot the chicken. If everyone followed my advice, I announced, they would not only have more fun but also produce more creative and nourishing fare for their customers.

I jumped down from the podium and placed one crown on a female head and another on the nearest male. "In my hotel," I said, "you will always be king and queen, and you will always pull the strings." I then gave each of the crowned heads a string to pull.

They yanked at the strings, opening the curtain to reveal members of the next panel. Laughter and applause filled the room. The speech was such a success, I was asked to give a similar talk at the Tallahassee Chamber of Commerce in Florida.

On my way to the airport I realized to my horror that I had forgotten my rubber chicken. Panicked, I said to the driver, "I forgot my rubber chicken."

He looked at me strangely in the rear view mirror, then turned around and drove back to the house. Helga was waiting in the driveway, holding my rubber chicken.

Late, I rushed through airport customs. The U.S. immigration officer wanted to know what was in my carry-on bag. When I opened it up, out popped the rubber chicken. The officer stared at it a moment, looked at me, cocked an eyebrow, and yelled, "Next!"

Chapter Sixteen

Our award-winning director of convention services, Freddy Kippert, was one of the Sheraton's show cards when it came wowing a convention. Freddy, without question, was a prima donna and we locked horns many times, but he knew his business; one of the best. Many times he saved the conveners from themselves, finding a solution when no one else could.

Freddy arranged the best staff Christmas parties. The planning would begin in June, and if Freddie decided you were part of the show, you were automatically drafted onto the 80-foot-wide stage he constructed. Rehearsals started in September and were kept top-secret. We sometimes had a cast of 80 singing and dancing in a production that rivaled anything seen on Broadway.

One year I suggested we open up the show and perform it for senior citizens. Goldie Brass at Shoppers Drug Mart arranged to give out tickets. John Ryan, the owner-operator of our tour and travel desk, provided a couple of buses to transport seniors to the hotel. The Toronto Transit Commission gave us free tokens for those coming by public transit. As soon as CFRB radio announced the party, our switchboard lit up. We'd never seen anything like it. The tickets were gone in less than 24 hours.

I contacted everyone who was anyone in the city—the premier, the lieutenant-governor, the mayor, the chief of police, television and film stars, TV anchors. Just about everyone we contacted showed up to be seated with a Sheraton staff member and eight seniors at each table. Even Santa arrived, pulled by a real reindeer, surrounded by a half dozen kids, my two sons among them.

Finally, the lights dimmed, the music started, and the show began. The audience had a grand time. When the final curtain came down and it was time to leave, there were lots of hugs and kisses for our staff. It was overwhelming to hear how much this meant to people. A couple of times I had to leave the room in order to pull myself together, filled with memories of my mother and how lonely she must have been in Germany with us living in Canada.

There were many special moments like this during the Sheraton years. Moments of laughter and tears and time seeming to fly past. The changes we made, the ideas, innovations, the opportunities, and the family that somehow grew up in the midst of it all—thank goodness for Helga!

Memories.

This mammoth hotel in the center of Toronto had been a great training ground, not just for me but many others as well.

My friend Tord Smidt, who assisted Kai Herbranson in Canada and the U.S., moved back to Sweden with his wife Malou. After managing the Grand Hotel of Stockholm, Tord eventually bought his own hotel, the Radisson SAS Hotel and Conference Center in Stockholm.

Kai Herbranson retired to Scottsdale, Arizona. Executive chef Hans Behrends became assistant vice president of food and beverage at the Sheraton head office. Eventually, he went on to become general manager of a hotel in Australia and then managed hotels throughout Asia. He retired to Victoria, Australia. Hans Behrends' assistant, Leo Schuster, took over as the Sheraton Centre's executive chef, and later worked for Donald Trump before building his own beautiful country inn and then retiring to British Columbia.

Food and beverage director John Williams left for New York

City to become the number two man at the St. Regis Hotel. He recently retired as senior vice president for Europe, Middle East, and Africa for the Fairmont Hotel Resorts chain. He resides in Victoria, British Columbia.

Nan Palmer, our human resources director, moved up within the Sheraton Corporation and ended up running the Atlantis Resort in Nassau, Bahamas. She too is now retired. Klaus Tenter left to join the Four Seasons Hotels chain and then retired after 28 years with the company. Josef Ebner is now vice president at Toronto's Delta Chelsea Hotel. We see each other at least once a month at the Baker's Dozen, a luncheon attended by a group of downtown Toronto hotel managers. Catherine McAuley, who joined me on my next venture, is now back with Starwood Hotels and Resorts looking after global sales. Tim Lilleyman is vice president of operations at the Toronto Congress Centre.

But all that came much later. Back in the 1980s retirement was the last thing on anyone's mind, including my own. After 11 years at the Sheraton, it was time to go. The biggest and most important adventure of my life lay just ahead.

I had known Dr. Hans Abromeit and his wife Anna since 1972 when they regularly stayed at the Hyatt Regency Hotel commuting between Germany, the U.S., and Canada. An elegant couple, intelligent, sophisticated, and generous, we had become friendly and stayed in touch.

The Abromeits' offices, Lehndorff Group of Companies, were close to the Sheraton Centre so they frequently dropped by for lunch. Their business was commercial real estate investment. Over the years, they had been very successful purchasing thousands of apartment units, shopping plazas, and office buildings across Canada and the U.S., investing billions of dollars mainly with German, Austrian, and Swiss partners.

In 1982 they bought the Sutton Place Hotel. Opened in 1967, the 200-room hotel, with an additional 200 luxury apartments, had become dated. Yet it possessed an admirable history and continued to attract an eclectic clientele with its fine dining facilities and famous rooftop lounge, Stop 33. It also attracted a certain notoriety after the girlfriend of one of the apartment complex's occupants, fraudster Michael Myer Rush, planted a bomb underneath his bed. Only the high quality of the hotel mattress saved his life.

The Abromeits initially asked me to work for them in 1982. I was enjoying life at the Sheraton and declined. In 1986, they approached me again and this time made an offer I could not refuse—managing director and president of VIP Hotels Limited. The position included another property in Vancouver. What's more, the Abromeits were looking at expanding their hotel division.

Saying yes opened the door to the most exciting and, in some ways, the happiest and most rewarding years of my life—albeit the most professionally stressful. Making the decision to join the Sutton Place required Helga's approval as well as our sons Ralph and Stephan, particularly since the job would mean moving into an apartment in the hotel.

Stephan was at Ryerson studying tourism, while Ralph attended the University of Western Ontario in London, majoring in business administration. There were also two dogs to contend with, Lady, our Irish Setter, and Wolf, a German shepherd. Giving up our lovely home in Don Mills was one thing, giving up the dogs was something else again.

The boys already envisioned inviting over their friends and calling room service. They eagerly encouraged me to sign on. For Helga, giving up the dogs and her garden and her proximity to work was painful. But she, too, saw the opportunity to advance in my career.

As for me, I had concerns about running a hotel by myself. Having held executive management positions for more than 15 years, I knew better than anyone that now the buck really would stop at my doorstep. I had always wanted a room at the top. Well, here was the top, and it was scary.

Kai Herbranson, Sheraton's area vice president, had watched

my progress over the past 11 years and knew my talents as well as my shortcomings. He pronounced me a hard worker, honest, creative, aggressive, talented, and open-minded. "Just do it!" he urged me.

I decided I was ready for the biggest challenge of my professional life.

Chapter Seventeen

When I arrived at the Sutton Place, the new owners already had made some changes, updating the guest rooms, creating the main floor dining room, Sanssouci, and the cozy-yet-elegant Alexandra Bar. The idea was to reposition the hotel and to that end we adopted the theme "Tradition and Technology"—warm, friendly, professional services based on European hospitality, integrated with the latest technological innovations.

A renovation program promised great improvements to the hotel but over the years, ironically, it also hurt business. Constant noisy and dirty interruptions from jack-hammering—the vibrations caused coffee cups literally to dance on the saucers—nearly eliminated business on the lobby and second floor levels and hurt restaurant traffic.

Computerizing our already elevator-challenged hotel was one of the biggest and most frustrating hurdles. Guest complaints were constant. Even I could read the beautiful lips of Oscar-winning actress Marlee Matlin who is deaf, and know that she was fed up waiting an eternity for an elevator.

The creation of the second floor conference center was

one of the things we did right, along with pursuing the budding entertainment market in Toronto. Thanks to the focus we put on that business, it soon became responsible for a third of our room rentals.

In order to court show business, we reduced the number of rental apartments and increased the rooms to 208 with an additional 72 suites, ten on the 18th floor complete with kitchen cabinets filled with Royal Doulton china, silver cutlery, and our own engraved crystal glassware. Wash basins with gold-plated fixtures were installed. We added the finest linens, antique furniture, original oil paintings—anything and everything the visiting movie star might require, including an en suite Jacuzzi. The floor even had its own butler, Werner Jankowski, who soon became an essential part of our success.

In the midst of all this, I moved Helga and our two sons into a large apartment on the 25th floor with a wrap-around view of the city. Our Irish Setter found a loving home with friends Jean and Larry Iron. The German shepherd was returned to the breeder. Letting go of the dogs was difficult for all of us.

From the day I started in April 1986, I found myself working virtually around the clock. Helga saw little of me other than lightning appearances for a shave, shower, and change of clothes. I wore an average of two suits a day. My wardrobe, by necessity, expanded greatly and so did Helga's. Our social calendar quickly filled. Sometimes the hotel chauffeur would whisk us off to two or three events a night.

Getting to know the Sutton Place team was another challenge. As they do in any business, internal politics play a large part in the running of a hotel, from the organized union staff members— some of whom had been around since the hotel opened—to the various levels of management. It did not take long to figure out the strengths and weaknesses of the players as well as the various agendas. Overall, I came to the conclusion that we had a great professional team.

Repositioning an older, independent hotel in the market isn't necessarily difficult as long as there is a history, and the public knows this is a fresh start. We certainly had history on our side, but Toronto was going through a renaissance with many new hotels offering exciting features and customer loyalty programs backed by the deep pockets of big corporations.

Being an independent hotel, even one with a great reputation, can be a disadvantage. If you travel to Timbuktu and have the choice to stay at the Timbuktu Inn or the Sheraton Timbuktu Hotel, where would stay? In the 1980s and 1990s travelers tended to stay with what they knew—branding became all-important.

Eventually, the Sutton Place became part of the German Kempinski Hotel chain, a division of Lufthansa Airlines. The added muscle of a big corporation would provide a competitive edge—at least that was the thinking. Unfortunately, Kempinski wasn't much help. In fact, just about all they provided was the name of a character on a beloved TV show.

Jim Henson, creator of the Muppets, stayed with us for a two-year period while producing his *Muppets* TV show. A tall, quiet, polite man, he noticed new stationery and match books featuring this curious-sounding name, Kempinski. It caught his fancy to the point where he named one of the show's characters Hans Kempinski. I could hardly object. When he finished taping the season, Jim gave me my very own Kermit the Frog watch.

Hans Kempinski was the only enduring part of our association with the German hotel chain. The relationship failed basically because Kempinski shifted its expansion plans away from North America. And then to make matters worse, Lufthansa and Kempinski parted ways. We needed someone to represent us in so-called feeder markets such as Montreal, Calgary, Vancouver, New York, Washington, D.C., Boston, Miami, Los Angeles, and Chicago. That task was partially accomplished by a company called the Leading Hotels of the World, brilliantly run by by president and CEO, Joe Giacoponello.

With reservation, marketing, and sales offices as well as an association with hundreds of the best hotels around the world, they brought us eight percent of our annual business, offering a prestigious window to the wider world. Yet not far away, my competitor, Klaus Tenter, general manager at the Four Seasons Hotel, woke up every morning knowing that the corporate reservation system delivered 45 percent or more of his transient occupancy.

Being on our own forced us to hustle a lot harder than the guy up the street. I was always trying to come up with ways to make ourselves stand out, to stay competitive—something unique that would serve as a door opener, a memory jogger.

I glued a brand new Canadian loonie on one side of lacquered cards, the Sutton Place information and telephone number on the other, and distributed the cards at foreign trade shows announcing, "Here is your first Canadian dollar to come and visit us."

I sent out letters with a new quarter glued to top of the page— the cost of a pay phone call in those days—asking prospective customers to give me a call. When I followed up, most people invariably remembered the Canadian quarter.

Guest comment cards are a vital part of getting feedback from

Front left: Sir Peter Ustinov, Cardinal Emmett Carter,
Mrs. Anna Abromeit. Rear left: Douglas Bassett,
Dr. Hans Abromeit, me, John McGreevy.

your clients, but the survey cards were hidden away in the drawers where no one ever saw them. I created a new survey with a shiny penny attached, saying: "A penny for your thoughts and a dollar for the Sick Kids Hospital." Response was immediate and produced a large annual donation at the CTV Sick Kids Telethon. Courtesy umbrellas constantly disappeared, so we told guests the umbrellas belonged to the Sick Kids Hospital. If they wanted an umbrella, we would add a $10 charge-donation to their room bill. It worked.

But we always needed more, and the burgeoning local movie industry went a long way toward helping us achieve that. During the years I was at the Sutton Place, Toronto film production grew from a meager $50 million to a $1.5 billion business.

At the beginning though, there was no business. Thanks to three men and a baby, that all began to change.

With Eric Braeden, star of TV's
The Young and the Restless.

Chapter Eighteen

Three Men and a Baby was based on a popular French film, *Trois Hommes et un Couffin*. Rewritten by a young Canadian screenwriter, James Orr, along with his partner, Jim Cruickshank, the comedy starred Tom Selleck, Steve Guttenberg, and Ted Danson, a trio not exactly at the height of movie stardom.

The unlikely director was Leonard Nimoy, better known as the Vulcan Mr. Spock from *Star Trek*, than for

his work behind a camera. Nevertheless, *3 Men and a Baby* went on to become one of the biggest hits of the era and helped establish Toronto as a destination for runaway Hollywood production.

Not only did the cast stay at the Sutton Place for three months, several staff members ended up as extras in the film, and everyone in town talked about the private dinners the co-stars hosted every Thursday in Ted Danson's Royal Suite, the largest in the hotel.

Leonard Nimoy and his wife Susan Bay.

The swirl of publicity surrounding *3 Men* considerably raised our profile. Before long we were entertaining any number of movie stars. The joke was that you could see more stars at the Sutton Place than in Hollywood. Tom Selleck would saunter into the dining room casually dressed in shorts with his shirt open to display that famous chest. As he passed, he put his hand on my shoulder in greeting. The woman I was dining with nearly fainted.

Soon the media named us the premiere star-spotting destination in town. We had to be careful when it came to hiring staff because so many potential employees just wanted to get into positions that would give them access to our famous guests. We zealously guarded the privacy of the celebrities staying with us, particularly from the growing army of freelance photographers known as *paparazzi*. They lived or died on photos they captured of stars caught unawares at hotels such as the Sutton Place.

The hotel occasionally played a character in the productions being filmed in Toronto. We became New York's Helmsley Palace so that actress Suzanne Pleshette could play Leona Helmsley, the world's most notorious hotelier for a TV movie titled *The Queen of Mean*.

Even I briefly got into the celebrity act when executive producer Michael Sloan set a segment of the *Kung Fu* television series starring David Carradine at the Sutton Place. It featured that internationally renowned actor, Hans Gerhardt. I still have the director's chair with my name on it.

Ah, fame. How fleeting it is.

Tom Cruise checked in to film *Cocktail*. Protecting his privacy became the most important aspect of his stay. We promised his agent we would ensure he was not bothered. However, we couldn't stop the word getting out that he was at the hotel. Fans and autograph seekers crowded the lobby hoping for a glimpse of the young superstar.

Cruise, meanwhile, remained in seclusion in our largest suite, surrounded by family members, rarely stepping out in public. That

Executive Producer Michael Sloan
presents me with my own director's chair.

didn't stop one female fan who managed to check into the suite next to his. Not only did she not meet her idol, she left without paying the bill!

Maintaining a celebrity's privacy wasn't always easy. Jane Fonda, in town to shoot *Stanley and Iris* with Robert De Niro, loved riding her space-age bicycle dressed in a traffic-stopping fluorescent-colored bodysuit and helmet, oblivious to surprised guests realizing this weird-looking person in wrap-around sunglasses carrying a bike was the world's most popular female movie star.

I took Kathleen Turner to a Paul Simon concert, arranged for Jane Fonda's husband, Tom Hayden, to throw the first pitch at a Toronto Blue Jays game, hosted German actor Armin Mueller-Stahl, his wife Gaby, and son Christopher at a polo match. Sam Neill joined me for a tennis match with John McEnroe, and I arranged for soap star Eric Braeden to play a celebrity tennis match with Monica Seles and Gabriela Sabbatini. When Burt Reynolds and Tom Cruise wanted to watch more NFL games, we hoisted a special satellite TV dish onto the roof to accommodate them.

Celebrities often joined me for Sunday brunch and, of course, there were any number of dinners at the Chef's Table, which for a time was the hottest ticket in town. The Chef's Table was simply a table set in the middle of the kitchen where the chef's team usually dined. We transformed it into a unique experience that everyone who was anyone wanted to be part of. Executive Chef Niels Kjeldsen and his team would prepare as many as 10 samplings of seasonal dishes, accompanied by a selection of wines chosen by master sommelier Hector Vergara.

The ascendancy of the Toronto International Film Festival (TIFF) only contributed to the sense that if you were a movie star

My friend Dusty Cohl.

in Toronto, the Sutton Place was *the* place to stay. By the mid-1980s the festival had become the largest single cultural event in the city. It had virtually taken over the downtown core and we were very much a part of it—thanks largely to Dusty Cohl, a Toronto lawyer who was the cowboy hat-wearing co-founder of the festival (along with Bill Marshall and Henk van der Kolk).

It was Dusty who helped me and my sales team convince Helga Stephenson, Piers Handling, and Michelle Maheux of TIFF to make the Sutton Place the festival's official headquarters. Dusty and the *Toronto Sun's* entertainment editor, George Anthony, invariably holed up in a suite at the hotel during the festival.

I kept coming up with new ideas involving celebrity guests, thereby keeping the hotel in the local spotlight. Jack Lemmon was in town shooting producer Michael Brandman's TV version of Eugene O'Neill's *Long Day's Journey into Night.* Production had fallen behind schedule forcing Lemmon to stay in town over Thanksgiving. Knowing the importance of that holiday to Americans, I hosted an old-fashioned dinner with turkey and all the trimmings. Lemmon took charge, slicing turkey for guests, as affable as the characters he often played in the movies.

When legendary director Norman Jewison premiered his latest movie *In Country* at the festival, we mounted a culinary salute featuring vegetables from Norman's farm in Caledon, north of Toronto. Items on the menu were named after his best-known pictures. For example there was a borscht soup for *The Russians Are Coming.* Scampi prepared in a pernod and garlic sauce was titled *The Art of Love* (one of Norman's first films). The *Rollerball* was a filet wrapped in bacon served with a light pink peppercorn sauce. Norman was particularly proud of his maple syrup. When King Hussein of Jordan and his wife Queen Noor stayed with us, I sent them Canadian Maple syrup candies and cookies along with a maple leaf-shaped mini-bottle of Norman's syrup.

As they were leaving, Hussein thanked me and presented me with a watch and fountain pen embossed with the royal crest. He asked if he could buy more of the maple syrup he and his wife had come to love.

Sharing a laugh with King Hussein of Jordan.

"How much would you like?" I asked.

"One hundred gallons," replied the king.

Gulp. Where was I going to find that much maple syrup on such short notice? Then I thought of Norman. Turns out, not only did he make great movies, he could also come up with 100 gallons of his maple syrup for the King of Jordan.

I often thought of Hussein and his wife sitting around their palace in Jordan, pouring Norman Jewison's maple syrup over their breakfast cereal.

One of the regulars at the hotel was actor Eric Braeden, an international sensation as Victor on the popular TV soap opera, *The Young and the Restless*. He was introduced to me by talent agent Lilana Novakovich.

Braeden was born in Germany the same year as me, just an hour away in Northern Germany. His uncle lived in Itzehoe, the city where I grew up. As a child Eric often visited. Who knows? We may have played in the same sand box. We became friends, and any time he was in town we always tried to get together.

I took Eric, Bernd Bohl, the hotel's operations manager, and my son Ralph to the official opening of the SkyDome (now Rogers Centre). Once the camera spotted Eric and threw his face up onto the Jumbotron screen, he was mobbed for autographs. When he tried to leave, he found himself pinned against a wall by eager fans. The police had to be called to escort him out.

When word got out that Eric was dining in the Sanssouci Restaurant, dozens of teenage fans descended. They had been attending two different Bat Mitzvahs in the hotel. I made a deal with them. If they left us alone so Eric could have dinner in peace, we'd drop in on their celebrations.

They agreed. After finishing a much quieter dinner, we went up to the function rooms were the Bat Mitzvahs were being held. The mob scene was incredible. Everyone wanted a picture. When he danced with one of the Bat Mitzvah girls, her mother shoved her aside and embraced Eric.

Another time, we decided to surprise a friend of ours who was an intense fan of Eric's. She opened the door at 11 p.m. to find the man of her TV dreams standing there with a red rose and a bottle of Dom Pérignon. She almost fainted. But so did just about every woman who met Eric.

Loni Anderson and Burt Reynolds
at the time of their engagement.

During the time Burt Reynolds stayed with us while shooting two movies, he proposed to his long-time girlfriend, Loni Anderson, an actress who was not only a beautiful woman but also incredibly elegant and very kind.

In advance of the proposal, Burt decided he wanted the atmosphere inside their suite to be more romantic. Hotel butler Werner Jankowski was sent to buy all the roses he could get his hands on. Vases of flowers were placed around the suite, the bed strewn with rose pedals. Loni, it should be noted, said yes.

Later, I was in the elevator when Burt entered. Two women got on at another floor. As soon as they saw the two of us standing there, their eyes brightened. I could sense Burt stiffening beside me.

"Mr. Gerhardt!" cried out one of the women. Burt looked at me. Both women went on about how exciting it was to stay at the Sutton Place. On they went until we reached the lobby. The elevator doors slid open and Burt Reynolds said, "After you, ladies."

They barely acknowledged him as they exited. One of the women stopped.

She glanced back at Burt. "No, it couldn't be," she said. The two women continued on.

Burt and I traded knowing glances. "Hans," he said ruefully, "you are bad for my ego."

When actress Joanne Woodward was in town doing a stage production of *Sweet Bird of Youth* at the Royal Alexandra Theatre, her husband Paul Newman came to stay for six weeks. They were a lovely, elegant couple yet very quiet. Their children and relatives visited frequently, but otherwise they spent a good deal of time by themselves, wandering around the city, recognized but not bothered.

I didn't have much to do with them, but one day I watched as Paul and Joanne came into the Sanssouci for a late lunch. Two businesswomen about to leave spied the passing Newmans. "It's Paul Newman!"

Paul politely turned and gave them one of the smiles that had made him a movie star.

The woman were momentarily mesmerized. Then one of them called out, "Paul."

He turned again.

"Nice ass."

Cool Hand Luke just smiled.

*Paul Newman and wife Joanne Woodward
dine at Sanssouci.*

*Bernadette Peters, Peter Allen,
signing the wall at the Chef's Table.*

*Introducing Armin and Gaby Mueller-Stahl to
Tony Bennett.*

Chapter Nineteen

I'm often struck by the odd combination of celebrity I encountered at the Sutton Place. Violinist Yehudi Menuhin was introduced to Professor Ernö Rubik, the man who invented the Rubik's Cube. The first man to scale Mount Everest, Sir Edmund Hillary, met singer-songwriter Leonard Cohen and later, actor Eddie Albert.

Lorne Greene, Ben Cartwright himself from the long-running *Bonanza* TV series, swapped stories with singer Roger Whittaker. Author James Michener sat with Canadian literary legend Morley Callaghan at the annual Writers Guild dinner—the two of them enjoying each other immensely. Actor Tony Curtis dined with retail legend and theater producer Ed Mirvish. Runner Ben Johnson enthusiastically snapped photos of *Young and the Restless* star Eric Braeden.

Tom Cruise and Michael J. Fox were smaller than I imagined, whereas Tom Selleck and Ted Danson were both taller. Then again, Professor Rubik did not look like a Rubik Cube, and James Michener did not strike me as one of the bestselling authors of all time.

When actor Tony Danza checked out of the hotel, I introduced him to hockey superstar Wayne Gretzky, who was just checking in. There was Tony, a scar on his face, in a T-shirt and jeans, looking like a hockey player shaking hands with Gretzky, tanned, in a suit and tie, looking like a movie star.

Introducing Tony Danza to
Wayne Gretzky.

Wilt Chamberlain, the basketball legend, stayed with us and declined a longer bed saying he had learned to adapt to a shorter world. Not all guests were so easily accommodated. Pop singer Prince arrived for a private visit with his entourage and security at the same time Governor General Jeanne Sauvé got there with *her* entourage and security. We also had provincial and federal government officials meeting with a German trade delegation. Everyone in the world seemed to have a stretch limo that had to be parked.

As though we didn't have enough problems that day, Ben Johnson appeared for a press conference, scheduled in the wake of accusations of his steroid use setting a world record at the Olympic Games in Seoul, Korea. Worrying about the media circus around Johnson, Prince's privacy, the Governor General's entourage, and the security of the international trade missions was enough to drive a lesser mortal to drink.

Jane Fonda, besides her movies, also had a flourishing career as a fitness guru. In order to satisfy her desire for daily workouts, we outfitted one of the rooms in her suite with wall-to-wall mirrors, special lighting, and all kinds of fitness equipment. Actor Robert Mitchum's travel coordinator insisted on changing the ensuite bathtub for a step-in shower stall. Even so, Mitchum disliked the suite and changed rooms.

Director Harold Becker, while filming *Sea of Love* with Al Pacino and Ellen Barkin, stayed in a non-smoking suite on the 18th floor for three months. He neglected to tell us about his love of cigars. The suite had to be fumigated, but even so you could still smell his cigars. Becker refused to pay for the cleanup and even put a stop on his final payment. It wasn't until I confronted him during a visit to Los Angeles that he agreed to compromise on costs.

It wasn't just cigar-smoking directors we had to contend with. Entire productions ran out of money and collapsed. Stars such as Richard Burton and David Niven could not save their movies while filming in Toronto. Peter Fonda and Nastassja Kinski, co-starring in a film that collapsed in mid-production, left us with an unpaid bill of $30,000.

Actor Donald Sutherland, a regular, had trouble checking in one night when his credit card was rejected. The night manager finally registered him, but I heard about it the next day from Sutherland himself. My profuse apologies did not help. He never stayed with us again.

Not all the problems came from our famous guests. On occasion their spouses could be much more difficult—and you ended up gaining an unwanted insight into a celebrity marriage. I

Prime Minister Pierre Elliott Trudeau signs our guest book.

managed to be part of a break-up that started when the celebrity couple argued over dinner. She threw a glass of wine in his face and then slammed the glass down, cutting her hand on the broken glass. Not long after, they separated.

Prime Minister Pierre Trudeau loved a glass of milk and an oatmeal cookie before retiring. We always had it waiting for him in his suite. For Charles Bronson, it was a boiled egg. The last of over 100 films Bronson made was *Death Wish V* shot in Toronto. Hollywood columnist George Christy recommended the Sutton Place. He assured Bronson we would take good care of him. He insisted on only one thing: a daily breakfast egg boiled for exactly three minutes.

We never seemed to get it right. Every time we met, he'd say, "Hans, how long does it take to boil a three minute egg?" Eventually, we boiled an egg in his suite, timed it, and got it right.

Bronson was known to be taciturn and difficult, but I found him to be quiet and private, and I always got along with him. However, when you're trying to run a hotel and deal with difficult celebrities, not everyone is going to like you. A case in point was the actor David Carradine.

Carradine stayed at the Sutton Place on and off for the four years he was shooting a reboot of *Kung Fu*, the TV series that

With David Carradine and
Robert Lansing
on the set of Kung Fu.

originally made him a star. Since then, Carradine's career had been up and down. A kind and talented man, sadly, he and his partner drank too much, too often. Finally, I told the series producer, Michael Sloan, that I didn't want Carradine in the restaurant and bars.

Carradine apparently didn't get the message. The next day he came into the bar accompanied by a Russian wolfhound on a leash. He was told that he would not be served alcohol. He sat for a time and then asked for me. When I walked in and saw the dog, I thought it best to keep my distance. I told Carradine we didn't allow dogs in the bar. He tried to hand me the leash.

"You take him out of here and get me a drink," he said.

When I refused to take the dog or get him a drink, he jumped to his feet, glaring at me. I wasn't sure what to expect. He turned, dropped his pants, and mooned me right there in the bar. After a few seconds he straightened, pulled up his pants, and walked out, head held high, the dog at his side.

That was not the only time I was mooned. Steven Tyler, band leader of Aerosmith, and his drummer Joey Kramer, checked in one evening. They did not arrive quietly. When the staff on duty failed to calm the rockers, they called me. I came out and asked them to cool down. They both looked at each other, nodded, and as they made their way to the elevator, pulled down their pants and let everyone in the lobby have a look at their bare buttocks.

All in a day's work.

The actor Bruce Dern, best known for playing psychopaths and villains in movies such as *The Wild Angels* and *Black Sunday*, rushed off the elevator one afternoon, frantically waving at me.

"You got a thief in your engineering department," he shouted. "I just caught him and got my wallet back. He isn't going to try that again with me!"

I calmed him down and listened to his story. He had left his suite, realized he forgot his wallet, and returned to find a maintenance man attempting to fix his air conditioning unit, even though no one had reported it broken. His wallet wasn't on the credenza where he had left it. He demanded the maintenance man give it back, otherwise all hell would break loose. Bruce Dern threatening to break all hell loose gives you pause. Even so, the maintenance man claimed he had not taken the wallet.

Dern leveled that malevolent stare he used on John Wayne just before he killed him in *The Cowboys*. That did it. The maintenance man dropped the wallet and ran for it—out of the room and right out of the hotel, never to be seen again.

With Henry Mancini.

Chapter Twenty

Veteran British actor Trevor Howard was best known for co-starring in David Lean's *Brief Encounter* and for playing Captain Bligh to Marlon Brando's Fletcher Christian in the 1962 version of *Mutiny on the Bounty*. As fine an actor as he was, Howard was renowned in show business circles for his drunken escapades.

When he came out of retirement to play opposite Loretta Young in a TV movie titled *Christmas Eve*, he checked into the Sutton Place. The producer asked us to remove any alcohol we found in his suite.

That task was assigned to butler Werner. He would check Trevor Howard's room daily, removing the bottles of vodka he found. Howard never seemed to catch on, but then again, neither did Werner's daily intervention do much to staunch the flow of vodka.

One day Werner invited Howard into his suite where the two of them proceeded to get into the sauce. Eventually, Howard stumbled off to the washroom, passing shelves groaning under the weight of vodka bottles. Howard stopped to peer at the bottles. The initials T.H. were attached to each bottle. Howard inquired as to where Werner got all the booze. Werner told him that they belonged to the actor. He became furious. How dare Werner take liquor from his room. He was a guest of the hotel. He was not a child.

Later, it was Werner's turn for the bathroom. When he returned, there was no sign of Howard. However, his hat and sports jacket were still in the room. Fearing the worst, Werner rushed out to the balcony and looked down 18 floors. He couldn't see anything.

Werner checked Howard's suite. He wasn't there, either. Around 1:30 in the morning, he called me. "Hans, sorry to bother you," he said. "But I think Trevor Howard fell over the balcony."

I sat bolt upright in bed, instantly awake, envisioning the next day's international headlines: "Toronto Hotel Kills Noted British Actor."

In case of emergencies, I always kept a track suit, running shoes, a flashlight, and a set of master keys next to the bed. Within minutes I was dressed and down in Werner's suite. Security meantime searched the hotel. No sign of a famous drunk actor.

I ordered a review of security camera tapes to see if they picked up any sign of him. We were searching through the tapes when on the lobby monitor we saw two police officers enter the hotel with a flushed and angry Trevor Howard in tow. The officers had found him across the street at Bistro 990 pounding on the locked door, demanding to be let in at two in the morning.

We had not killed off one of the world's great actors, after all. To the contrary. By the next day, all had been forgotten if not forgiven. Butler and star had bonded. Besides, Howard was now aware that Werner had the key to the vodka stores.

I frequently hosted a house table during our Sunday brunch, inviting a mix of outside guests and long-term hotel clients. Howard was playing a butler in *Christmas Eve* and by now Werner had become his technical advisor. The two of them arrived together from the set and joined us.

Howard forgot to take his hat off. As he sat down, Werner swiped it off his head. That made some of the old actor's hair stand up. Werner, like a mother, gently patted down the errant hair strands. It was funny, and rather touching, to see the two of them interact together.

Twice Werner tried to get Howard home to England. The first time they ended up in a restaurant and forgot Howard's flight. The second time they were actually driving to the airport when Werner observed that this was the highway to Niagara Falls. Howard said that he had never been to Niagara Falls. Werner could hardly believe what he was hearing—Trevor Howard could not possibly leave Canada without seeing Niagara Falls!

They missed that flight as well. Once again, Howard's long-suffering wife was left waiting across the ocean for her husband's return.

On the third attempt, he finally made it, probably because we sent him off to the airport and kept Werner at the hotel.

Sometimes a famous guest was a pleasant surprise. By the time Marlon Brando stayed with us while making *The Freshman* with Matthew Broderick, he had gained an enormous amount of weight and was barely recognizable. Nonetheless, despite a fearsome reputation for being difficult on a movie set, he turned out to be a wonderful guest. Whenever we encountered each other he always said something in German.

Shortly after Brando arrived he asked Werner the butler to order a side of smoked salmon and put it in his fridge. Werner knocked on the door with the salmon. When there was no reply, he entered the suite with his pass key.

He gasped out loud and almost dropped the salmon tray.

Brando, dressed in a track suit, lay in the middle of the living room on his back, eyes closed. Werner thought he'd had a heart attack. Then Brando cracked open one eye. Meditating, he explained.

One night the fire alarm went off at three in the morning. This was before loud speakers were installed in the rooms, so any time the alarm sounded, guests had to vacate their rooms and take the

Marlon Brando ready for a scene in The Freshman *with our butler, Werner Jankowski.*

fire stairs down to the lobby.

Dressed in his usual track suit, Brando arrived to find the lobby full of sleepy guests in an assortment of nighttime attire. He took one look around, then found a seat at the concierge desk and proceeded to take over, directing fellow guests to the washroom, answering their questions. The amazing thing was, no one recognized him. As he guided people around, I passed the desk.

He gave me a wink.

Another early morning fire alarm brought the comedian Jerry Lewis down to the lobby. He wasn't quite as helpful. "This had better be a real fire to get me out of bed at this time of the night," he yelled at me.

He was trying to be funny.

One of the nicest actresses we ever had stay with us was a young unknown named Sandra Bullock who was in town to film an episode of *Bionic Woman* starring Lindsay Wagner. This was long before she became an Academy Award-winning superstar. Such a beauty, not just in looks but also in her personality. It turned out we had a fair amount in common. She was German-born, her mother's name was also Helga, and her grandfather was, like my father, involved in the German rocket program during World War II. Who knows? Maybe Sandra Bullock's grandfather knew Hans Gerhardt's father.

*Richard Anderson with
the then-unknown
Sandra Bullock.*

Norman Jewison, Gregory Peck at the premiere of
Other People's Money.

Jerry Lewis with wife SanDee.

Eddie Albert (sitting) Professor
Ernő Rubik (of Rubik's Cube fame), Alan Eagleson,
Donald Rickerd, and guests.

Chapter Twenty-one

Ontario Premier David Peterson hosted a luncheon for the ambassador of a Far Eastern country. Since it was a cold November day, everybody was rushed into the lobby from their limousines. The premier greeted the ambassador and his wife and the lunch was a great success. Then the ambassador's wife started looking for her mink coat. When she couldn't find it, everyone started getting nervous. The premier whispered to me: "I need this problem solved."

I assured him it would be taken care of. The premier was a good customer and we had a great working relationship.

The staff checked everywhere without finding the mink. By now the ambassador's wife was becoming impatient. The fur coat, recently purchased in San Francisco, was brand new and irreplaceable.

Having done business with furrier Alan Cherry, I called and asked if he could lend me a fur coat for a day or two.

"No problem," he said. "Send her over."

No sooner did she arrive at his store than Alan called me back, upset. "Hans, are you crazy? She picked a coat and wants us to cut a foot off."

If he altered the coat, not only would it belong to me, but I was going to have to pay for it in advance.

I could hear the woman's voice in the background shouting about how badly she had been treated at the hotel. I made an executive decision and asked Alan to give me a deal.

"Ten thousand dollars cash and its done," Cherry said.

We rushed over a certified check and the ambassador's wife had her very own altered Alan Cherry fur coat. Meanwhile, we continued to look into the case of the missing mink. The checkroom concessionaire swore she never saw the coat and so did the concierge. From what anyone could recall, it had been taken back to one of the cars. Which car? No one could remember.

Warmed by her new mink, the ambassador's wife returned to Ottawa two days later without saying a word to us. When our corporate insurance adjuster got wind of what I had done, I received a good lecture about insurance policy matters when it came to giving away $10,000 fur coats.

The insurance adjuster tried without success for six weeks to get in touch with the ambassador's embassy in Ottawa. Finally, I got a call from the embassy's consul-general in Toronto, demanding a meeting.

I hurried over to his office, arrived on time, and then was kept waiting for the next hour. When I was finally ushered into the consul-general's presence, he refused to shake my hand. Instead, he ordered me to sit down and then paced back and forth, loudly accusing me of insulting his ambassador and his country, implying that I had lied about the fur coat—we had lost it, now we were trying to cover up. As soon as he finished his tirade, he turned on his heel and left—without even saying goodbye.

We were about to drop the whole matter when we got a call from a prestigious Ottawa furrier demanding a down payment on a $27,000 fur coat the ambassador's wife had ordered. The insurance adjuster and I agreed this was war. No way were we going to pay for another coat. An investigator discovered the missing fur had been purchased in San Francisco all right, but seven years ago, and the ambassador's wife had haggled the price down to $4,000. Not exactly irreplaceable.

I telephoned Premier Peterson's office and told him what had happened.

"You did the right thing," Peterson said.

At the premier's urging, we sent the ambassador a letter pointing out that his wife was now in possession of a $10,000 fur coat, altered to her specifications. These were the facts. The ambassador could either dispute them or keep the fur coat and we would call it even.

We never heard another word.

For years a woman in her 80s, blind in one eye, a chain smoker who loved vodka, resided on the 24th floor, directly below my apartment. She would come down for lunch and sit quietly in a corner. Then she came with a cane and after that, a walker. Eventually, she relied on a nurse who would bring her in a wheelchair. Finally, she could not leave her apartment and we delivered lunch to her.

When I toured around the hotel, I would always drop by her apartment to see how she was doing. Often I added a flower and a note to her luncheon tray. It became clear that she had only day care and was alone in the evenings. As she smoked her cigarettes, she would burn her fingers and drop the butts on the floor, leaving burn marks all over her carpets. I warned her that she had to be more careful but it didn't do much good.

Smoke detectors were not yet mandatory, nonetheless we encouraged residents to install them. She did not want to buy one. I told her not to be surprised if Santa dropped one off. The next day we installed a smoke detector in her apartment.

Not long afterward, I was taking one last stroll around the hotel in the evening. I arrived at the door of our 25th floor apartment hearing a "beep beep" sound coming from somewhere. Increasingly nervous, I called security. The beeping was a smoke alarm, and it was coming from the old lady's apartment. I hurried downstairs, met the security man on duty, and pounded on her door. No answer. As soon as we got the door open, we were hit by a blast of black smoke. I set off the fire alarm and then the security man and I stumbled inside. We found the old woman unconscious in the darkness and managed to carry her to safety. Of course, it turned out she had fallen asleep on the couch while smoking and set the place on fire. She was all right, but it did teach her a lesson. No more smoking and drinking.

Early one morning when we were the headquarters hotel for Tennis Canada's Men's Tournament, one of the star players called down to the front desk complaining about the couple next door who were loudly and repeatedly making love.

The night manager called the room and asked the occupants to be quiet. Soon the noises started up again. The tennis star, angrier than ever, lodged another complaint. This time the night manager went up to the room. The couple promised to keep it down.

Shortly thereafter, they started up yet again, even louder than before. By this time the tennis player was so upset the night manager called me. Easier, I decided, just to move the player to another suite. I went up to apologize on behalf of the hotel. As we talked, the noise from the next room began rising to a truly impressive crescendo. Enraged, the tennis player yanked open his side of the connecting doors and hammered against the other door, yelling for the couple to shut up.

A moment of silence followed. The other door swung open, and there stood a stark-naked man with a full erection.

"Can I be of help?" he inquired.

I had to hold back the tennis player. The last thing I saw as the naked man closed the door was an equally naked woman smiling from the bed, throwing kisses at us.

We quickly moved the tennis player to another suite. The next day he lost his match and checked out without a word to anyone.

On another occasion, walking through the lobby, I encountered a young man sitting in one of the easy chairs smoking a joint. Not quite believing what I was seeing, I went over and told him he could not smoke illegal substances in the hotel.

Unperturbed, he politely asked who I was. When I told him I was the manager, he immediately put out the joint. That was the end of that.

Or so I thought.

The next day housekeeping delivered a note addressed to me found in one of the rooms. "Dear Mr. Gerhardt," it read. "Thank you for stopping by to remind me not to smoke in your beautiful lobby. I always appreciate the elegant ambiance and fine service you provide. As it happened, our conversation was overheard by a nearby lady seated with a business partner. Once he left, she came over and asked me if I had any more joints. I did. And now I am finishing breakfast in her suite."

Sometimes you help your guests in the most unexpected ways.

Harry Ornest, who owned the Toronto Argonauts, stayed with us for an extended period. He would regularly stop by our restaurant, have a cup of coffee for $1.50, leave a 50 cent tip, and take the day's newspapers, worth $8. Then he would go outside and take the complimentary house car to his office. All for a lousy $1.50—plus tip!

At the end of the day, he came back to the bar, loaded his pockets with peanuts, and then left without so much as buying a beer. Following several attempts to stop it by our manageress, Lydia von Paal, I talked to him, offering these services for a fee. He politely declined, announcing he would take his morning business elsewhere since I could not afford to do business with him. Not long after, he checked out—without paying the last month's rent.

The life of a hotelier.

On the other hand, a lovely couple, Queenie and Benjamin Luxenberg, couldn't have been better residents. They actually interviewed me at their mansion in fashionable Rosedale before moving in. Mrs. Luxenberg was a tall, elegantly-dressed lady in her 80s. Her husband was a few years older, always wearing a three-piece pin-striped suit and vest with a gold watch on a gold chain across his chest.

What a pleasure it was to see them around the hotel and listen to them talk about the great life they lived. Queenie told me about a present she gave Benjamin on his 75th birthday while vacationing at their private club. Admiring the stunning young swimming instructor, Benjamin mused that he never learned to swim. Queenie bought him swimming lessons for his birthday. Benjamin and the swimming instructor spent the next six hours together. Afterward, he said with a twinkle in his eye, he still could not swim.

One day we were having lunch with actor Roscoe Lee Browne and his friends from New York. The Luxenbergs were seated at the next table. One of Roscoe's friends said she had never been to Toronto before, even though she always wanted to come after meeting a stylish lady from the city at a party in the Hamptons on Long Island.

Having bought a one-of-a-kind cocktail dress for the Hamptons party, she was surprised to see another woman arrive wearing the identical dress. Then, to her astonishment, a third woman walked in wearing the same dress. The third woman took one look at her two rivals, turned on her heel, and left. Roscoe's friend and the other woman laughed together and congratulated each other on their great taste.

They promised to stay in touch, but Roscoe's friend had lost her card. The only thing she could remember about the lovely woman in the same dress was that her name sounded like a country.

I had a sudden thought. "Luxenberg?"

Roscoe's friend looked surprised. "Why, yes. I think that's what it was."

I excused myself and walked over to the Luxenbergs and asked Queenie if she recalled the afternoon at the Hamptons. She certainly did, thought that it was one of the funniest moments of her life.

I waved over Roscoe's friend. Even before she reached the table, she recognized Queenie from that afternoon 20 years before. I filed that away under "Six Degrees of Separation."

*Helga, Richard Anderson, his Royal Highness
Sultan Ahmad Shah of Pahang.*

Hosting an art show with Tony Curtis.

Chapter Twenty-two

Actor Richard Anderson, best remembered for co-starring on TV's *The Six Million Dollar Man* and *The Bionic Woman*, was a friend of producer Michael Sloan. They worked together on several shows and I got to know Richard during his time in Toronto. When Helga and I came to Los Angeles, Richard invited us to dinner and then a drink at the Polo Lounge in the Beverly Hills Hotel.

As we sat in the lounge, an Asian gentleman arrived at our table. He had an invitation from Sultan Ahmad Shah of Pahang, Malaysia. His Royal Highness wanted us to join him for a drink. Richard had been a guest at the sultan's palace in Kuala Lampur during a celebrity tennis game. The sultan and his two sons, along with an entourage of 20, were on a North American polo match tour. The horses traveled in their 747 Jumbo Jet while His Highness and family moved about in a 737.

The sultan had been in Canada a couple of times and was friends with former Prime Minister Pierre Trudeau. However, he had never visited Toronto. Not one to lose an opportunity to promote the hotel, I urged him to stay at the Sutton Place when he came to town. He asked me to send him a brochure. I assured him that I would. Did the sultan have a business card?

Silence at the table. I had asked a *sultan* for his business card?

Ahmad Shah broke into a smile. "Funny," he observed, "when they made me a king, they failed to give me a business card."

The next morning, Richard picked us up in his 1936 antique Ford Phaeton convertible just as Sultan Ahmad Shah and his entourage were about to leave for a Malaysian Day festival in a park near Rodeo Drive and Wilshire Boulevard.

Enamored of Richard's antique car, he insisted on sitting behind the wheel while a police helicopter buzzed overhead and a small army of police cars and motorbikes waited. He invited us to join in the celebration and when we said we would, told us to follow the convoy. Lights flashed, sirens screamed, the helicopter churned over the sultan in his bullet-proof limousine while we followed behind in a TV star's classic convertible. Welcome to Hollywood.

At the park, hostesses, beautifully dressed in their national costumes, seated us. Hostesses explained the various dishes being offered. The sultan, with Helga on his right, and Miss Malaysia on his left, cheerfully translated. Possessed of a great sense of humor, he reminded me of Bob Hope. His English language skills were perfect. He dressed in western clothes, obviously enjoyed life in America, and was a bit of a star gazer, having invited several to his palace for celebrity tennis and polo matches.

I noticed that Ahmad Shah never ate but passed the food to his minister of defense or a second stern gentleman who appeared to be his food-taster. Obviously he wasn't taking any chances.

The leaders of the group of seven industrialized nations were meeting in Toronto. After a great deal of lobbying both in Toronto and Bonn, I managed to arrange for the German delegation to stay at the Sutton Place.

Due to the unexpected announcement of a federal election, Chancellor Helmut Kohl and his wife, Hannelore, skipped their Ottawa visit and arrived in Toronto a couple of days early.

*From left, actor Edward Woodward, Helga, me,
Mrs. Hannelore Kohl, Ralph, at the Chef's Table.*

In contrast to the imposing figure of the chancellor—he must have been well over six feet and at least 275 pounds—Mrs. Kohl was around five-foot-six, in good physical shape, an attractive woman with a warm smile.

Whenever the chancellor and Mrs. Kohl left the hotel, I made sure I was there to say goodbye and to greet them when they returned. I must have made an impression. One evening Mrs. Kohl arrived back earlier than her husband. She asked me if I had a twin brother since whenever she opened the door, there I was. I assured her there was only one of me. She laughed and asked how I found time to spend with my family.

As a matter of fact, I said, I was having dinner in the hotel kitchen with my family and some friends. Intrigued, she wanted to meet Helga and our son Ralph. "But just for a second," she said.

Two hours later we were still sitting there. Mrs. Kohl, Helga and Ralph, producer Michael Sloan, and his wife, actress Melissa Sue Anderson, co-star of *Little House on the Prairie,* everyone listening raptly as British actor Edward Woodward recited Shakespeare.

Mrs. Kohl, quite fluent in English, seemed very much at home among these strangers, ignoring the four security guards hovering nearby. The German people adored her and called her by her first name, Hannelore. It was easy to see why she was so well liked— down-to-earth and always looking at you straight in the eye. As we would say in German, she was very *sympathisch.*

The next day, while her husband attended the G7 conference, I took Frau Kohl to the rooftop ballroom to show her the city skyline. Spotting the CN Tower, she said she would love to visit. I urged her to go. When she said she didn't have an interpreter, I suggested Helga accompany her. Wonderful, she said.

They had a great time particularly when they arrived at the observation level and found a tour group from Germany. They recognized the chancellor's wife who chatted with her fellow countrymen and cheerfully posed for photographs. Sadly, Hannelore developed a strange allergy to light and virtually lived in the dark until her death in 2001. Helga and I really enjoyed our time with her.

The first president of the Czech Republic, Vaclav Havel, arrived in Toronto wearing a plastic belt that broke just as he was about to go out. He asked me for a stapler to fix it. Astonished that the president of the Czech Republic wouldn't have a proper belt, I offered him mine. He gladly accepted it, promising to give it back after the luncheon.

I told him to keep it. And he did.

When Prince Philip arrived for a visit, I escorted him to his suite. Entering the sitting room he immediately went over to the windows and threw open the curtains to get a better look at the city. He asked about a couple of buildings that had gone up since the last time he visited and then leaned forward, peering at the glass. "Haven't washed the windows lately, have you?"

I was in shock; the husband of England's Queen had noticed our dirty windows. *Quel embarrassment!* I turned and saw the twinkle in his eye. We both had a good laugh. The Duke of Edinburgh had a sense of humor after all.

A long time patron of the Outward Bound program, the Prince was honored later that day at a luncheon I co-hosted. Well-known Newfoundland artist David Blackwood donated a painting that was to be presented to His Royal Highness. It sat on a easel covered by a black velvet cloth until a waiter accidentally knocked it over and cracked the frame.

I jumped up, told the waiter to give me a hand, and together we carried the painting out of the room and straight down to a neighboring frame shop. The framer demanded to know how much time he had. Thirty-three minutes, I said.

He fixed it in 30. We got the painting into the room as Prince Philip started his speech. He paused when he saw me replacing the painting on the easel. Here, he said, was a great example of the Outward Bound program in action. With me taking a bow, everyone in the room laughed and applauded.

Not everyone was quite as popular as German chancellors and British Royalty. When Slobodan Milosevic came to power as president of Yugoslavia following President Tito's death, the country was thrown into turmoil. Tito had ruled with an iron fist. When Milosevic, a Serb, took over, the various fractions started to revolt.

As he arrived in town, greeted at the airport by a large unruly crowd, security was high. Outside the hotel, barricades went up as riot police on horseback and in patrol cars moved to control thousands of demonstrators who had gathered across the street. I was told to meet Milosevic inside the hotel in order to minimize his public exposure.

Moments before the president's motorcade arrived, I got a call on my radio that there was a bomb threat. Police with bomb-sniffing dogs immediately searched the building. A hoax as it turned out, but it had the effect of increasing the tension we were all feeling.

As soon as the president appeared, the demonstrators began screaming and pressing against police lines. Mounted officers fought to keep the crowds back as he was rushed into the lobby.

As I greeted him, Milosevic seemed shocked by the anger of the crowd. Everybody, including his entourage and RCMP security, squeezed into a waiting elevator so that we were practically nose to nose.

The doors closed. We did not move. I groaned inwardly. I was stuck on an elevator with a man who would soon become known as one of the world's most murderous dictators. I glanced over at Milosevic. He was about my size but not very fit, and rattled, aware of the bomb threat, and now finding himself trapped in this metal box. Beads of sweat popped out on his forehead. Everyone was wearing winter overcoats. Finally, it got so warm that each of us in turn gingerly removed our coats.

One of the Canadian government officials at the back started to hyper-ventilate. We managed to pry open the doors a couple of inches so he could get some air. That calmed him. Hotel security finally realized that the elevator was stuck but couldn't figure out which floor. We had lifted up enough to disappear off the lobby elevator panel display. Fortunately, an Otis elevator repairman was in the hotel. Ten minutes later the repairman managed to start the elevator moving again. It had seemed an eternity. Milosevic was still perspiring as he exited.

Chapter Twenty-three

Visiting Los Angeles, George Christy, the fabled *Hollywood Reporter* society columnist, took me to dinner at Wolfgang Puck's restaurant, Spago.

I was in L.A. staying at the Bel Air Hotel where general manager Kerman Beriker arranged a suite for me overlooking the gardens. Sitting on the porch outside my suite, I could see the actor Robert Wagner visiting his mother who lived at the hotel.

George, for many years a regular guest at the Sutton Place, had arranged a dinner in my honor at Spago, the hottest restaurant in town. My fellow dinner guests included British comic actor Dudley Moore, who showed up with his fiancée, Brogan Lane. Also present was actor Robert Stack and his wife Rosemary, and actor Spiros Focas who had a part in *The Jewel of the Nile*.

Wolfgang Puck lived up to his reputation; the meal was delicious, the restaurant full of very important people. A wonderful evening. Wolfgang even signed one his cook books for me. Robin Leach dropped by our table. He hosted *Lifestyles of the Rich and Famous*, an immensely popular syndicated television show that celebrated just what its title suggested. I loved the show and asked Robin to come down to Rio de Janeiro in December for the annual gathering of the Leading Hotels of the World. Robin asked me to send him details and gave me his business card.

"That will never happen," said Dudley, the cynical observer of all things Hollywood. I bet him that Robin would be in Rio for the convention. The bet came down to this: if Robin did come to film it, Dudley would have to play the piano at the Sutton Place. If Robin did not come to Rio, Dudley would stay at the hotel for free whenever he was in town.

A few months later, just as he had promised, Robin flew to Rio with me. Dudley indeed would play the piano at the hotel.

Someday.

Legendary Hollywood journalist George Christy.

In Toronto, George Christy is celebrated for the annual luncheon he has hosted for over 25 years as part of the film festival. His friends Michael Budman and Don Green, founders of Roots, originally sponsored the affair held at the Four Seasons Hotel. George restricts the guest list to no more than 60, ensuring that it remains one of the festival's hottest tickets. George doesn't just let anyone in; therefore, *everyone* wants in.

He is a demanding perfectionist dressed up smartly as a courtly charmer. Once I hosted a lunch for him at the Sutton Place. There were only 10 of us, but George insisted on taking command of the preparations.

When the luncheon was over, he showered me with compliments about the food, the service, the charming guests (including actress Cheryl Ladd), and the beautiful ambiance of the Sanssouci. Surprised, I blurted out, "George, it was my *pressure*."

Dusty Cohl, George Anthony, and, in particular, Brian Linehan, never let me live that down.

And Dudley Moore?

It took four years to work out the dates, but finally Dudley agreed to play three nights at the Sutton Place. The concerts sold out in a day.

In the meantime, composer Henry Mancini arrived in town for a concert with singer Cleo Laine and her husband, the musician and bandleader, John Dankworth. Over dinner with them, I mentioned Dudley Moore's impending visit. Cleo smiled and said, "Just a moment here." She opened her briefcase and pulled out a CD she and Dudley had recorded together.

Cleo explained that Dudley used to play piano in John's band and was their tenant for a time in London. Wouldn't it be wonderful, I suggested, if Cleo and John could surprise Dudley at his concert? It worked out even better than that. Dudley arrived from Colorado, changing planes in Detroit where Cleo and John had performed the night before. Ironically, they ended up on the same plane to Toronto where I was waiting.

Kurt Gebauer, John and Cleo's long-time manager, hurried out of the baggage claim area. Dudley was being held up by immigration, he announced. Cleo and John were trying to help but to no avail. In the rush to get Dudley to Canada, I'd neglected to secure a work visa for him. The prospect of sold-out shows and no Dudley Moore abruptly became a real possibility.

Thankfully, the immigration people turned out to be Dudley Moore fans and eventually let him into the country. We celebrated over dinner with a bottle of Niagara wine. Dudley was surprised at the quality. He never thought that wine grapes could grow in our otherwise harsh climate.

The next day we drove to Niagara-on-the-Lake, the pretty little community in the heart of wine country. Driving together, I discovered that Dudley was allergic to, of all things, the sun. He lived in California, in that sunniest of places, Venice Beach, and yet he had to avoid the sun.

We toured my friend Don Ziraldo's Inniskillin winery, guided by Debbie Pratt. From there we drove to Niagara Falls. Walking over to view the Falls, we encountered a couple of hundred Japanese tourists. Their tour guide did a double take when he saw Dudley. All we could understand was "*Arthur*-movie-Dudley Moore." That was enough to set off 200 camera flashes. The crowd closed in excitedly.

"Do you want your picture taken or do we make a run for it?" I asked.

Run, decided Dudley. The Falls then witnessed the curious spectacle of a small English movie star being chased up the street by a delighted swarm of Japanese tourists.

With Cleo Laine, John Dankworth,
Dudley Moore, and Helga.

For Dudley's show, a turntable was set up with a concert grand piano on it so that the audience would be no further than 35 feet away. He had studied classical music before becoming a comedian, and was an accomplished pianist. After I introduced him, he performed various classical and Broadway pieces along with his own compositions, the show punctuated with the comedy that had made him famous.

Two thirds of the way through the performance, to the delight of the audience, Cleo Laine and John Dankworth appeared. It was one of the most memorable evenings at the Sutton Place, and I think of it any time I am reminded of Dudley. He had a dry, deadpan sense of humor, was genuinely appreciative of what we did for him, and was fascinated by Canada.

He died tragically in 2002 at the age of 67 from complications resulting from a degenerative brain disorder. My fond memory of him is of a friend who enjoyed his success yet never found real happiness in his personal relationships. Maybe, too, he was disappointed that his musical talent was largely ignored. Whenever I think of him, though, I remember that afternoon in Niagara Falls, and I smile.

Dudley Moore was not the only great pianist to play the Sutton Place. The internationally renowned Byron Janis once gave an impromptu performance in the kitchen. So did composer and album producer David Foster. When she was just starting out, Diana Krall played in the hotel bar for $650 a week. Of course she would not lift the keyboard cover for that today. What a talented lady. She was so quiet that often no one noticed her, except of course for the way she played a piano. She was supposed to play background music, but when she was on the keyboard, the music was very much in the foreground.

One other famous pianist occasionally played at the hotel. Actor Christopher Plummer would stay up all night, his eyes closed, endlessly tinkling the ivories. He was pretty good, too.

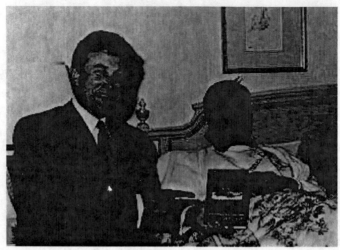

In bed with humorist Dave Barry.

I wanted Oscar at the Sutton Place. Well, what I was really after was a photograph of the iconic Academy Award statuette filled with the names of all the stars who had stayed at the hotel. Butler Werner Jankowski and I posed in formal dress on either side of a blow-up of Oscar, tipping our top hats under the headline, "Thinking of You."

The ad ran in the *Los Angeles Times* and trade publications. I received an "honorary" Oscar nomination in the *Times* for the most creative ad. However, our advertising agency wanted nothing to do with it knowing Oscar was trademarked by the Academy of Motion Picture Arts and Sciences, the body that sternly oversees the awards. The agency made me sign a release absolving them of any responsibility.

Sure enough, a registered letter soon arrived from the legal department of the Academy asking me "not to think of Oscar again." Well, I thought, at least they had a sense of humor. I agreed to behave.

A couple of years later, my sons Stephan and Ralph, both living in the U.S., saw an ad sponsored by the Academy in which all nominees' names appeared in a replica of the Oscar statuette promoting the forthcoming awards show—the same ad that got me into trouble.

I wrote the Academy a letter saying that while they had asked me to stop thinking about them, they obviously did not stop thinking about me. I never got a reply. However, I did see an article in which the "creator" of the Oscar ad talked about the difficulty of coming up with new ways to promote the Academy Awards each year.

No mention of my name anywhere.

Ontario's chief of protocol, John Latimer, introduced me to his son Jeffrey, who had started to produce shows in Toronto.

Jeffrey asked if I would be interested in hosting the legendary George Burns in exchange for promotional considerations. Definitely, I said, anxious to have the 90-year-old comedian and actor at the hotel.

George Burns.

Before Jeffrey could get a signed contract, Burns' agent required assurance that the hotel could properly accommodate him. I wrote a letter promising that while George Burns stayed with us he would get the best suite in the house, any dietary needs would be accommodated, and I would personally be available to him and his staff.

The next thing I knew, George was on his way to the Sutton Place.

The advance media coverage was terrific. However, ticket sales were slow. I got hold of my old friend Paul Godfrey, who by this time was publisher of the *Toronto Sun*. Unless disaster struck, Paul promised to have Burns on the front page of the Sunday paper.

Burns agreed to have his picture taken as soon as he arrived. My friend Peter Kircher loaned us his fire-engine-red 1989 Porsche Speedster anniversary edition, and Paul Godfrey arranged for two beautiful Sunshine girls to be in front of the hotel as Burns' limo pulled up.

Getting the legendary comedian out of the limo was no problem, but then we had to squeeze him into the tight confines of the Porsche. Easier said than done. We did it one leg at a time, wrestling as gently as possible with a frail nonagenarian. In the midst of all this, a throng of people burst out of the hotel, leaving a Bar Mitzvah. They stopped dead when they saw who was half in and half out of a bright red Porsche. George Burns himself! They were uncontrollable.

Burns' agent, who wasn't much younger than his boss, swung into action. He told me to get a blanket, a wheelchair, and a vodka martini, straight up with three olives. By now the temperature had dropped. Burns got out of the Porsche, shaking, looking a bit confused. Meanwhile, everyone on duty at the hotel pitched in to help keep the crowd back until we finished the photo shoot.

After that, we got Burns into the wheelchair, wrapped him in the blanket, and handed him the martini. There was one more picture. Tom MacMillan, general manager of the *Sun*, a lifelong Burns fan, insisted on being photographed with his idol.

As soon as the photo was done, Burns sipped his martini without spilling a drop. Immediately, he stopped shaking. Inside the hotel, where it was warmer and quieter, he relaxed and smiled, holding his martini in one hand, an unlit cigar in the other. I think he had vastly enjoyed the little circus.

He demanded to know who I was and thanked me for the assistance, not knowing I was probably responsible for the melee. The next morning I hosted a brunch in my suite for Burns with guests Ken McGowen, George Cohon, founder of McDonald's Canada, and his wife, Susie.

Burns, with a big grin, chided me for almost killing him in the cold Canadian weather. However, looking at the *Sun* front page with him sitting in the red Porsche convertible surrounded by beautiful women, he agreed the discomfort was worth it. I presented him with a $100 cigar courtesy of a local cigar maker. He appreciated the gift, although he confided he would never pay that kind of money for a cigar. We spent a wonderful hour together. The whole time, I never saw him stand. "I only stand when I work," he cracked. "That's when I get paid."

Then it was back to his suite for a rest before the show that night. For 55 minutes he sang and danced, told jokes, and basked in the glow of unending standing ovations. Later that evening, I sat beside him at a dinner party celebrating his agent's wedding anniversary. Only later, when I saw the photographs, did I realize how small he was. He made witty small talk until dinner was over, and the anniversary cake we provided had been cut—a tiny piece for George—then it was bedtime.

The following morning he left for L.A. I said goodbye in front of the hotel. "It was great to meet you," I said. "Only meeting God would be greater."

"Hey, I played God, remember?"

And so he did.

My boyhood idol,
German singer Freddy Quinn.

Goldie Hawn.

Clint Eastwood.

Kate Nelligan.

Chapter Twenty-four

Singer-songwriter Roger Whittaker was not only a regular guest at the hotel, he also became a good friend. As it happened, he had the same road manager as pop legend Rod Stewart. We were having dinner one night when who should drop by but Stewart himself, accompanied by his wife at the time, Rachel Hunter.

Marcello Mastroianni.

Roger, who looked relaxed and tanned, told us about the villa he'd rented outside Rome, next to one owned by the Italian actor Marcello Mastroianni. Every morning he looked to see if Senor Mastroianni was about but no such luck. There was never any sign of him. He was disappointed. He would love to have met the great star of *La Dolce Vita*.

I asked Roger to look across the room at a gentleman having dinner alone. "Roger," I said, "there's Marcello Mastroianni sitting right over there."

Mastroianni was in town shooting a movie called *Used People* with Shirley MacLaine.

I went over to Mastroianni's table. He had watched us from afar but had no idea who I was sitting with, had never heard of Roger Whittaker, let alone Rod Stewart. But he was most interested in the beautiful Rachel Hunter.

Mastroianni sauntered over and Roger finally met his Italian neighbor. Roger told Mastroianni about renting the villa right next to his. Mastroianni looked confused. He wasn't certain which villa Roger was talking about since he had one villa for his wife, a second set aside for his mistress, a third occupied by himself.

When Mastroianni discovered Helga was from Germany, he recalled doing a German-Italian co-production in 1957 titled *Sand, Love and Salt*, in which he had to sing. It was a stupid movie, he said. He was dressed in a fisherman's costume with a striped shirt and wide-legged pants. He had to sing in Italian and then, for the German audience, in German.

It was such a silly song he could never forget it. He then sang it to Helga. The great Mastroianni singing in German for her in Toronto with Roger Whittaker looking on—truly a night to remember.

A couple of days later, I was awakened by Werner the butler with the news that Mastroianni had been rushed to hospital. Celebrating his 70th birthday at the nearby La Scala Restaurant, he had forgotten to take his medication. He told me later that he made the mistake of eating the special risotto the chef prepared for him. The Italian chef was from Civitavecchia, near Rome. Mastroianni told him that he spent time there as a young soldier.

"Do I have a special recipe for you," the chef said. Mastroianni did not want to hurt the man's feelings, so he ate it all. It was not always easy to be an internationally loved and adored movie icon. The rich food and his lack of medication put Mastroianni in the hospital. All it took to bring the actor back to his old self was a major bowel movement.

*Meeting Sophia Loren my
first day on the job.*

Mastroianni's good friend and frequent co-star, Sophia Loren, happened to be staying at the Sutton Place the day I started. When I told her I was meeting my favorite movie star on my first day at work, she smiled and said, "Does this make me a virgin?"

I did something a hotel manager should never do: I blushed. The great Sophia was in town to shoot a movie titled *Courage*, based on a true story about a mother searching for the criminals who sold drugs to her addicted son. She looked stunning. Tall in her high heels, and self assured, she entered the suite like—well, like a movie star. I have to admit I was awestruck by her beauty and her persona. I had adored her ever since I saw her on the screen in Germany in the late 1950s, when I was still a teenager.

A couple of years later, Ms. Loren and her late husband Carlo Ponti returned to the hotel for the film festival. A press conference was scheduled across the street at Bistro 990. Her press agent suggested we walk. Not possible, announced Ms. Loren. She was in high heels made for looking impressive, not for walking.

Since the Sutton Place was now the film festival's headquarters,

I had persuaded company president Vic Doolan to lend us 12
BMWs so that we could offer free shuttle service to hotel guests
during the 10-day festival. They were lined up on the motor court.
I suggested we drive Ms. Loren over. That was fine with her.

The young driver was startled when a bona fide screen goddess
climbed into the back of his car—startled and very nervous. When
he started out of the drive to cross the street, he hit something and
badly scratched the front fender. Cue another BMW. Eventually,
we were able to get her across the street, although by the time we
did it, I was beginning to think crossing the Rubicon might have
been easier.

Toronto publicist Gino Empry was the little guy you loved to
hate. For years Gino was one of Toronto's most powerful
publicists. His clients included everyone from Tony Bennett to the
Irish Rovers. He also booked acts at Toronto's most prestigious
nightclub venue, the Imperial Room at the Royal York Hotel. Years
before, Gino represented Sophia Loren in Canada. But there had
been some sort of falling out. Gino was determined to get back
into her good graces.

He peppered me with phone calls. Was she at the hotel? He
had to know. When I refused to confirm one way or the other, he
camped out in the lobby prior to the gala presentation Ms. Loren
was due to attend.

Knowing there would be fans in the lobby, Ms. Loren wanted
to be rushed out to her limo and not stop for anything. A private
elevator brought her down to the lobby. We took the precaution
of opening both swing doors to the motor court so no air pressure
would mess the lady's hair (a good hotel manager thinks of
everything).

Gino, pacing in and out of the lobby, spotted the waiting
limo. He suspected it was for her and hurried back into the hotel,
entering through the revolving door just as Ms. Loren swooped
past. He saw her and desperately tried to reverse the revolving
door. Just then an equally desperate photographer slammed into

*Siegfried Jerusalem, me, Elke Sommer,
and Christopher Plummer*

the door and that sent Gino flying across the lobby. By the time he got to his feet again, Ms. Loren had sped away.

Undaunted, he somehow got to the University Theatre ahead of us. I have no idea how he did it, but there he was, his wig slightly askew, waiting on the red carpet to greet his favorite actress.

Ms. Loren even managed to look pleased—but perhaps wisely, she never allowed Gino to represent her again.

The Germans descended. Maybe it had something to do with my background. At one time my childhood idol, the German singer Freddy Quinn, was at the hotel as was actress Elke Sommer (*A Shot in the Dark, The Prize*) and her hotelier husband, Wolf Walther. The German operatic tenor Siegfried Jerusalem was also a guest.

Siegfried had dinner one night with Helga and myself, along with Christopher Plummer. Siegfried had performed on all the world's great opera stages and was celebrated as one the greatest Wagnerian singers. I wondered if he ever forgot his lines.

No, he replied, it had never happened to him, but he was onstage with another singer when he forgot his line. Instead of stopping the show, the actor sang to Siegfried in Italian, "I forgot my line." Siegfried, without missing a beat, sang the forgotten line back to him. The actor in turn sang back, "Thank you so much!"

The audience was none the wiser.

The next day Siegfried did a recital at the hotel. Thirty-five guests attended as he performed a number of arias. I sat in the last row with my back to the door. I could hear water running outside. I stepped into the corridor to investigate just as part of the ceiling collapsed and water sprayed down. I made sure the mess was cleaned up before slipping back to the concert. Siegfried caught my eye and winked.

After the performance, he shook his head, regretting he ever opened his mouth about never forgetting lines. When the ceiling crashed down, his mind went blank and for the first time in his long career, he couldn't remember the words. With no one to help him, he had to stop and start over again.

I suppose I can take small solace in the fact that any time one of the world's great singers remembers the time he forgot his lines, he thinks of me.

With David Foster on piano, John Williams, Brian Boitano, Katarina Witt, Sandra Bezic, and guests.

Chapter Twenty-five

These were heady years at the Sutton Place. I often reflected on how far I'd come—a poor child of the war who left school at the age of 15, an immigrant who came to Canada with a only few dollars and a pregnant wife.

I had traveled the world, met the poor and the rich, the unknown and the world famous. I'd escorted heads of state, stayed in the world's most luxurious places, flown in private jets, sailed on yachts, been entertained in vast mansions.

Stephan, Helga, and Ralph.

Through it all, I always tried to keep in mind that these perks I enjoyed so much were not mine; they were part of the job.

But I did enjoy them, no doubt about that. The kids had grown into their early 20s. Stephan, after studying in France, worked for a year in Germany making sales calls for Kempinski Hotels before returning to Canada and continuing his career at the Fairmont Banff Springs Hotel. He eventually moved on to Washington, D.C. to work in tourism at the Canadian Embassy. Ralph was pursuing a career in finance with BMO Nesbitt Burns. Later, after a stint at Shorcan, he joined Cantor Canada before moving to New York.

Helga was busy decorating our new home at the hotel and supervising the building of our dream home on Lake Simcoe.

The business continued to present all kinds of challenges. I was a first-time general manager overseeing renovations that seemed to go on forever, yet still having to deal with the day-to-day business of operating a major international hotel, taking care of guests, overseeing staff.

While average room rates had increased, so had operating costs. Occupancy rates were constantly challenged by new competitors. The early1990s were a constant struggle to stay on top of the business. But that was the job, and most days I loved what I was doing.

Once in a while, it even got me out of town.

Robin Leach in pursuit of the
Lifestyles of the Rich and Famous.

Since the Sutton Place was part of the Leading Hotels of the World, I attended its annual convention. In 1986 it was held in Rio de Janeiro, and I suggested to president and CEO Joe Giacoponello that we invite *Lifestyles of the Rich and Famous* host Robin Leach. This was the idea I had pitched to Robin when I met him along with Dudley Moore in Los Angeles.

Once I got Joe's okay, I contacted Robin. He loved the idea. A visit to Rio would allow him to feature breathtaking scenery, beautiful women, and great food, as well as rub shoulders with the representatives from the world's great hotels.

It was the Christmas season and one of the white tie galas took place at the home of the owner of the spectacular Copacabana Palace Hotel on Copacabana Beach. Guests were shuttled via deluxe buses to the residence and seated over the pool which was covered with acrylic glass. A buffet was served inside while we danced under the stars.

Four Seasons Los Angeles general manager Kurt Stielhack made the mistake of offering half of a $50 bill to our waiter. He promised him the other half if we didn't run out of champagne; we did not. We were a happy table.

Helga, a non-drinker, did not share our happiness or our jokes. When I loaded up my Swedish friend Tord Smidt's pockets with the host's gold-plated cutlery and tied a big red bow on his white dinner jacket, Helga was not amused. In sober retrospect, of course, I can see her point.

While we were sitting around with Robin one afternoon, he asked me if I knew Al Waxman, who, at that point, was riding high as the co-star of TV's *Cagney & Lacey*. I said I had known Al and Sara for years. Robin wanted to do a segment with them for another show he was producing, *Runaway with the Rich and Famous*. He was aiming for a February shoot in Toronto. I reminded him that it wouldn't exactly be Rio weather at that time of year. No, no, he insisted, the winter weather worked perfectly for what he had in mind—a romantic scene with Al and Sara on skates at City Hall.

Robin's visit to Toronto and a stop at the Chef's Table for dinner with the Waxmans, cemented our friendship. After that, we spoke often on the phone. When I heard a radio commercial for a travel service called The Last Minute Club that sounded suspiciously like Robin, I told him about it, and he threatened to sue. Rather than go to court, The Last Minute Club simply hired him to become their long-running spokesman. That association brought Robin to Toronto often, and resulted, based on my suggestion, in a *Lifestyles* segment devoted to the city.

It also brought Robin in contact with the Reichmann family.

The Reichmanns were Toronto developers who controlled Olympia and York, the worldwide real estate empire whose ventures included the Canary Wharf project in London. Stephen Reichmann, one of the sons of the three reclusive Reichmann brothers, had done business with us. In our conversations, Robin's name came up. Stephen, it turned out, was a fan of the show.

I knew that Robin wanted to interview the Reichmanns for *Lifestyles* but had been refused. I suggested to Stephen that he meet Robin on his next visit.

Robin arrived in Toronto from New York and Stephen Reichmann joined us for lunch. He teased Robin about all the freebees he got doing his series. "All you have to do is show the plane's logo and you get all the free tickets you need," he said.

Robin insisted that wasn't the case, and even showed him his paid-for New York ticket. Knowing that the Reichmanns had a fleet of private planes, and didn't exactly have to worry about air fares, I suggested that Stephen fly Robin to his next appointment in Boston.

"No problem," Stephen said. "Meet me tomorrow at one o'clock."

Robin thought he was kidding. He had been chasing the Reichmanns for an interview and here was one of the sons coming to him.

The next day it poured rain but nonetheless the Reichmanns' Challenger Jet was ready for take off. Robin still could not believe it. When Stephen left the aircraft to talk to the pilot, he grabbed me. "What is this Gerhardt? *Candid Camera?*"

We took off into the storm, as though the gods themselves would not dare threaten a Reichmann jet with Robin Leach on board. We rose above the dark clouds into an azure blue sky. As we did, the flight attendant popped champagne corks for Robin and myself—Stephen drank orange juice.

Robin clinked my glass and laughed, "Hans, *this* really is the lifestyle of the rich and famous."

I asked Stephen how the rest of the family might feel about taking an internationally famous TV star for a plane ride. Stephen considered the question for a moment, and then smiled.

"What are they going to do?" he said. "Fire me?"

Rome's l'Originale Alfredo di Roma Ristorante became famous in 1920 when newly married silent movie stars Douglas Fairbanks Jr. and Mary Pickford ate there. Owner Alfredo DiLelio

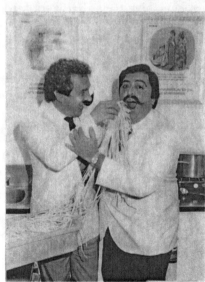

With the Real Alfredo III of Restorante Originale Fettuccine Alfredo and me as Alfredo IV.

prepared a special dish for the couple employing homemade fettuccine pasta served with a blend of herbs and tossed in butter and sprinkled with grated parmesan cheese. Although he had created the recipe for his wife in 1914, he had no trouble naming it after himself— Fettuccine Alfredo.

The restaurant became the couple's favorite stop in Rome. Before they left Italy, they presented Alfredo with a golden spoon and fork engraved "to Alfredo, the King of Noodles," and signed by both stars. From that day, the fork and spoon have been presented to the celebrities who dined there. Their photos line the walls of the restaurant.

In November 1986, I wrote Alfredo's grandson, Alfredo DiLelio III, asking if he would be interested in coming to Toronto for a promotion at the hotel. I never heard back. However, when I was in Rio de Janeiro, I read an article in the local English paper that he had just opened a restaurant at the Intercontinental Hotel on Ipanema Beach.

I called the hotel and they quickly connected me to his room. A sleepy Alfredo answered. I blurted out who I was, and that I had written him a letter but never received a reply.

He laughed. "You must be German," he said. "My wife's German and she talks non-stop too."

Thanks to that phone call, Alfredo agreed to come to Toronto. I had to buy his noodles, his secret butter, and his special cheese, along with his wine. Canadian government regulations prohibited the importation of the butter and I had to reimburse Alfredo for the five suitcases and the two hockey-size bags that it took to transport his noodles and cheese.

I arrived at the airport to greet him when his plane landed from Italy. All 360 passengers and crew left the plane. But there was no sign of Alfredo. Eventually, someone paged me to come to immigration. There was Alfredo holding up his famous golden spoon and fork, having pictures taken and signing autographs.

The problem turned out to be his female assistant. She was a "trainee" from Brazil and thus required a visa to enter Canada. We got it worked out and Alfredo finally arrived in Toronto.

Coming in from the airport, we were driving up University Avenue in downtown Toronto when I remembered that Mary Pickford's birthplace was nearby. Her house stood on what is now the Hospital for Sick Children. We pulled over so that Alfredo could read the plaque marking the site of the Pickford birthplace. He was touched. In a strange way, Alfredo's father and his brush with the two silent movie stars who inspired a world famous pasta dish, had come full circle.

My love affair with Ristorante Alfredo and Alfredo's grandson, continued years later when I dined at the Rome establishment with my old friend producer John McGreevy, who was traveling with Sir Peter Ustinov.

Sir Peter and John were in town doing a TV series about the Vatican. I was part of a trade mission led by Ontario Minister of Trade Monte Kwinter.

The photo of us taken that night is one of the larger ones in the restaurant.

For years, I lobbied the Leading Hotels of the World to hold their annual conference in Toronto, not an easy feat considering that previous conventions were held in places like Rome, Paris, Rio, London, and Singapore. Finally, with support from Four Seasons general manager Klaus Tenter, and Bill Crooke at the King Edward Hotel, Leading Hotels members decided to come.

While the three Toronto hotels shared official functions, the conference was held at the Sutton Place. I hosted president Joe Giacoponella, as well as Tord and Malou Smidt of Sweden's Grand Hotel, and Kerman and Kristina Beriker of the Beverly Hills Hotel. Sutton Place owners Hans and Anna Abromeit entertained with *Phantom of the Opera* star Robert Pilon—a magical night that was, ironically, the beginning of the end of another chapter in my life.

From left: Tord and Malou Smidt, Kerman and Kristina Beriker, me, and Helga.

Chaz and Roger Ebert.

Rod Stewart.

With Suzanne Pleshette and
Lloyd Bridges filming
The Queen of Mean.

Placido Domingo.

Chapter Twenty-six

The end came with the arrival of a Swiss newspaper article. Joerg Reichert, CEO of the North American Mövenpick Marché operations, told me about a story in *Die Weltwoche* critical of Lehndorff Group of Companies, founded and owned by my boss, Dr. Hans Abromeit.

The article accused Lehndorff of charging high administration and management fees even though returns to investors were low. In other words, Abromeit and his partners were doing fine; the investors weren't.

In the economic climate of 1992, even the conservative Reichmanns were suffering, having recently lost control of their London Canary Wharf project. If those canny operators were in trouble, where did that

Toronto Star *headlines Toronto's "hotel wars."*

leave the Lehndorffs? I began to fear the worst.

When the economy turns sour, the travel and the hotel industries instantly feel the pinch. The Sutton Place Hotel Kempinski (as it was now known), was facing increased competition, particularly from the new Intercontinental Hotel on Bloor Street. It had not only gone after our market share but also hired away several key middle management people.

In its sales pitch, the Intercontinental took great delight in pointing to our endless renovations. The criticism wasn't far off the mark. We had just completed a noisy and dusty garage reconstruction, and were starting to computerize the elevators, taking one elevator at the time out of service over an 18-month period.

At the same time as all this was going on, executives of the Hotel and Restaurant Union were under investigation for fraud. The union was soon replaced by the United Steel Workers, a tough bunch who demanded big changes to hotel contracts.

A provincial election resulted in the Sutton Place-friendly Liberals being tossed out of power in favor of the not-so-friendly New Democratic Party. The NDP government quickly directed business to cheaper hotels. At the same time, we lost 20 long-term apartment rentals from the outgoing Liberal MPPs.

Trouble was brewing in paradise. The hotel simply was not making money.

As Lehndorff's problems became known in the industry, the resulting rumor and speculation made Fuji Bank, the hotel's mortgage holder, very nervous. An accounting firm, Doan Raymond, was appointed to oversee Fuji's investment.

Then came one of those dates that is seared into my memory: November 26, 1992.

I had arranged a meeting with the president of Fuji Bank Canada, John Bailey. He brought along Doan Raymond's vice president of forensic accounting, Allen Berenbaum, and Lehndorff's vice president of finance, Stephen Lewis.

There had been an infringement of the agreement between

the bank and Lehndorff, John explained. Funds had been moved from the hotel to Lehndorff without prior approval of Fuji. Therefore, Fuji had called the loan and would take full possession of the hotel as of 3:04 p.m.

I was stunned. I knew things were not going well, but nothing like this. Mrs. Abromeit had been in the hotel at lunchtime telling the concierge she was disappointed that the lobby Christmas tree was not up. Nothing about a company about to implode.

John Bailey announced that Allen Berenbaum was now the hotel's receiver. Alan immediately stood up, opened the door, and called in Dale Lawlor. She would be at the hotel from that moment on directing all operations.

The Doan Raymond team was already outside my office, Dale explained. I would now report directly to her. No decisions could be made without her approval.

As I tried to digest all this, John Bailey offered me a package to stay on until the hotel operation was stabilized and ready for sale. Still reeling, I called Helga to tell her what had happened. Then I called a meeting of department heads to introduce Allen Berenbaum and Dale Lawlor. The next step was to address the staff at a general meeting.

Word had already spread; some staff members attended with tears in their eyes. Many had worked at the hotel all their professional lives. While I tried to give events a positive spin— Fuji Bank assures that our high standards would be maintained—the uncertainty in everyone's eyes was inescapable.

The news of the hotel's plight made the front page of the three Toronto newspapers. Not surprisingly, the international president of the United Steelworkers Union, Leo Gerrard, was soon on the doorstep to ensure the rights of his members. However, loyal non-union management employees, myself included, had virtually no protection under the bankruptcy. We had to fend for ourselves when it came to outstanding vacation pay and bonuses.

Clients became nervous, not believing our reassuring words that the Sutton Place would continue as usual. Catering and sales functions were cancelled at an alarming rate, resulting in millions of lost dollars. I did manage to convince David Nichol, the genius behind the President's Choice products at Loblaws, to co-sponsor a system-wide promotion for their famous Kobe sauce, importing Kobe meat directly from Japan. The hand-fed, beer-drinking Wagyu cattle received a daily massage in order to produce a highly marbled meat that sold for $100 a steak. Promotions like that helped keep us in the media spotlight and give the impression it was still business as usual.

But I was hurting. The salary package Fuji offered me was fine. But then Berenbaum over lunch, days before Christmas, wanted to renegotiate. Furious, I stood up and told him that I was calling John Bailey and resigning.

I had remained loyal in the critical aftermath of the hotel going into receivership, presided at staff meetings and media interviews, trying to reassure everyone that Fuji's interventions would help the hotel move on to a more stable future. This was the thanks I got?

He decided to leave my package alone.

The next thing, I received a call from Charles Grieco, chairman of the Ontario Hostelry Institute. I had been named Hotelier of the Year. Issy Sharp of Four Seasons was the previous recipient. Shortly after that, the Board of Governors of the International Tourism Association announced I was to be honored in Berlin for my global contributions to the industry.

At the same time as I basked in the glow of international hotel honors, I was trying to deal with suppliers who weren't getting paid by a young accounting graduate who had been put in charge of day-to-day decisions. That brought on more heated discussions. My relations with the receivers grew worse.

I have often asked myself why I bothered to stay. Most likely it was because I believed that I could help turn over a well-run hotel to more stable and seasoned owners. What's more, part of my deal included moving expenses and a small bonus receivable upon the final sale. In hindsight, the aggravation wasn't worth it.

Despite the stress and misery, I did have a moment when I just had to shake my head and laugh at the craziness of it all.

The moment was provided by a well-dressed gentleman who arrived in the lobby and announced he was the new owner. He inquired about various staff members, wanted to know their names, what they did at the hotel, and what they earned. When he heard the salaries, he shook his head. They were too low, he said. They would have to be reviewed.

One 70-year-old staff member was not so fortunate. The new owner fired her on the spot. She came to me weeping. I picked up the telephone and called the receiver. No, the hotel had not been sold. I got hold of security and we cornered the alleged owner and told him to get out. He genially wished us all a good day, and left.

I never saw him again but I did get a hand-written note offering to sell me the hotel for $1.

I resisted the impulse to take him up on the offer.

An ironic footnote to this whole mess: my nemesis, Allen Berenbaum, later was accused of "funneling" over $2 million from his clients. The company tried to keep the scandal quiet, and succeeded, until they decided to take possession of Berenbaum's Forest Hill house. That's when his wife Rochelle went public, making headlines that read, "Bay Street Trustee Steals Millions." She added that not only was a rapacious company trying to evict her and her children, but her husband was involved in an affair with his secretary.

I had to stifle the urge to send Mrs. Berenbaum flowers.

Finally, the hotel sold. Two years before it went into receivership, the Sutton Place had been valued at $90 million. It sold for less than $27 million to Macao billionaire Stanley Ho. His people had no interest in me, and, in fact, seemed downright suspicious. Hotel security kept a close eye on Helga, particularly when she loaded anything into our car.

As soon as the sale was complete, I left. Would I ever stay behind again after a hotel went into receivership? No. The whole process is just too painful.

My friends Ed Mirvish and Paul Godfrey.

Douglas Fairbanks Jr., Janet Leigh, and
Norman Jewison at a Variety Club reception.

Chapter Twenty-seven

The Old Mill sits surrounded by 1,000 acres of parkland along the banks of the Humber River in the west end of Toronto amid some of the most expensive homes in Canada. Yet it remains one of the city's hidden treasures.

Built in 1793 to mill lumber for home construction in York, it became a grist mill after a fire, then was abandoned after two more fires. A developer, R. Home Smith, began to develop the neighboring Kingsway area and used the grounds of the Old Mill to invite Toronto citizens to come by horse and buggy for tea and a little advertising. His motto for selling homes in the area was *Vallis Humbrea Angliae Pars Angliae Procul*—"A bit of England far from England."

A dance hall opened at the mill in 1914, the day World War 1 started. Soon it attracted returning soldiers looking for a place to dance and to meet girls. Today, it remains a traditional spot perfect for weddings (more than 800 a year) and families celebrating special occasions. Over the years ownership of the Old Mill changed hands a number of times before being acquired in 1991 by the father-and-son team of George and Michael Kalmar.

George was a successful realtor who assembled the land for

Toronto's Manulife Centre complex and later worked on the development of the newly created city of Bramalea. He also became a partner in the financially troubled Constellation Hotel located near the Toronto airport.

Buying out the original partner, George expanded the Constellation into an 900-room convention center that included a glass elevator. He also made sure he and his son had lavish suites, 5,000 square feet for him, 3,000 for his son. Well, he was the son, after all.

A widower, George often walked the halls at night with his Doberman, Max. One night he stumbled across one of his employees bent over the fish tank trying to catch a trout. George fired him on the spot. However, since Frank had gone to such lengths to catch his fish, George let him keep it. That was the kind of guy George was; he'd fire you for doing wrong but give you a break for showing some ingenuity.

Max the Doberman helped George sell the Constellation. The Regal Group of Hotels, based in Hong Kong, was on the hunt to expand into Canada. Two scouts from Regal checked into the hotel and began snooping around, asking questions. George got wind of their presence and summoned them to his office. He made sure Max was with him.

The two scouts found themselves confronted by a hotel owner, six feet four inches tall, weighing over 300 pounds, accompanied by a snarling Doberman. Nervously they admitted they were looking at the hotel as a potential acquisition. George and the Doberman both barked at them. George made more sense. He said the hotel was not for sale, and even if it was, they could not afford it.

The scouts inquired as to what the price they could not afford might be. George blurted out an astronomical figure: $110 million.

To his surprise, his visitors did not blink. They would check with their Hong Kong office and come back with an answer. The offer when it arrived was for $100 million. George ended up selling for even more than that, and he also negotiated a contract that allowed father and son to act as consultants for the next two years. And they could stay in their suites.

George and Max barked all the way to the bank.

Following the Sutton Place sale, Helga and I retreated to our home on Lake Simcoe to contemplate the future.

A move to Vancouver or Victoria, British Columbia was appealing. I thought of trying to establish myself out there as a marketing and promotion consultant. I sought advice from West Coast friends John Williams and Damien McGoldrick, who worked with me at the Sheraton, and former Hyatt colleagues Ian Barbour, Angus Wilkinson, Larry Belisto, and Franziska Kalteneggcr, as well as Ron Edgar, a transplanted Torontonian who owned a Chrysler car dealership in Victoria.

Also, by coincidence, I discovered that an ex-Sheraton chef, Leo Schuster, had relocated to Victoria where he established the Aerie Inn, ranked one of the top 10 North American inns by *Condé Nast Traveler*. He was a great help, as were my other friends.

But things developed slowly—too slowly for my liking. I spent weeks on the West Coast, leaving Helga alone on Lake Simcoe. That caused emotional strain for both of us. After nine months, I began looking around for other opportunities.

I had known George and Michael Kalmar over the years—they had tried to buy the Sutton Place while it was in receivership. It was during this period they first offered me a job. Even though they wanted to develop an addition to the existing 60-room inn, it still seemed like a come down after the Sutton Place. What's more, I would be working with a dominant father and son, and who knew how that would work out.

But as the idea of moving West faded, the Old Mill began to look more attractive. In March 1994, I called George to wish him a happy birthday. One thing led to another and before I quite realized it, I had become vice president of operations at the Old Mill.

As George and Michael shook hands with me, someone stole

my car from the parking lot. Helga had a feeling something was wrong. At the moment the car was stolen, she was trying to reach me on my cell phone, worried she had left her wedding band in the car's cup holder. It disappeared along with the car. Not surprisingly, parking lot security became a priority as soon as I started my new job.

I went to work assessing the strength, quality, and vitality of the Old Mill team. I reconnected with various movie and television contacts, including George Anthony, now a producer at the CBC, and CTV's president Ivan Fecan.

Soon, the Old Mill was being used regularly as a movie location. Ivan's wife, Sandra Faire, produced an Anne Murray Christmas special there. Nicole Kidman arrived to shoot scenes for a film called *To Die For*. Events in connection with the 20th anniversary of the Toronto International Film Festival were held at the inn. The stars of *Fly Away Home* attended a post-gala soiree. The film was based on the true story of a Toronto entrepreneur and sculptor who trained orphaned geese to fly South for the winter. On cue, a flock of geese swooped low over the guests on the patio. Festival co-founder Dusty Cohl turned to me and asked, "How did you arrange that?"

When you had been in the hotel business as long as I had, I told him, arranging for swooping geese was nothing.

My friend Peter Steinmetz's law firm, Cassels Brock & Blackwell, sponsored a reception hosted by Variety Village's Reg Bovaird, Freddy Gallaugher, and Al Dubin to fête TV personality Monty Hall and his brother Robert. The special guests that evening were three Hollywood acting legends: Douglas Fairbanks Jr., Janet Leigh, and Ann Miller.

At the same time as I sought star-laden events, I re-established the Old Mill's famous afternoon tea, started a weekly barbeque in the garden, reduced the stagnant 11-piece band to a more lively seven-piece group but continued the Old Mill tradition as Toronto's only nightly live dance venue.

I also introduced special events like the Hungarian Festival,

A Taste of Barbados, the Chocolate Lovers promotion, and a Valentine's Day celebration starring tenor Robert Pilon along with a 60-piece children's violin orchestra. The children, as young as six, dressed in tuxedos and looked adorable as they strolled between the tables.

Rediscovering the Scottish roots of the McGerrhardt clan resulted in my introduction of the annual Robbie Burns supper, a sold-out event to this day. Robbie Burns Day celebrations, as every good Scotsman—and a few who aren't—knows, is celebrated around the world on January 25 to commemorate Scotland's great poet, the bard of Ayrshire.

A Robbie Burns supper demands humor, song, and perhaps a glass or two of good scotch whiskey. Most of all though, a Robbie Burns celebration requires Haggis—sheep intestines stuffed with a sheep's heart, liver, lungs, and suet. The concoction is then spiced and boiled in the animal's stomach until it resembles a giant sausage.

Robbie Burns dinner at the Old Mill.

I was introduced as "Hans Ian McGerrhardt" from that far eastern Scottish shire known as Berlin. I was a fine McGerrhardt indeed, especially after a glass or two of the aforementioned scotch whiskey.

George and Michael had a unique father-son bond. At times of stress, I reminded Michael how fortunate he was to work with his dad. Not many of us are given the opportunity. At the heart of their relationship was a belief in doing what was best for the business, and nothing ever got in the way of that sensibility.

One time during a meeting, George misunderstood something said by the catering director, Helen Weech. He exploded, yelling and hammering his fist on the table—highly unusual for him.

When I tried to interrupt, he brushed me aside. Nobody could say a word, including his son. Michael had just bought himself and his father cell phones, the new rage. After a couple of failed attempts to halt his dad's tirade, he picked up his phone and punched out a number.

George's cell phone rang just as his enormous fist was about to come down yet again. He stopped in mid-air, picked his cell phone out of his pocket, and opened it. "Hello, who's calling?"

"It's Michael your son, and you are wrong dad," said the voice on the line.

Confused, George blurted, "Where are you, Michael?"

"I'm right here, dad. And you're wrong."

George looked over at his son, the two of them on their cell phones. Then they broke into laughter. They had that kind of relationship.

A biologist had found a rare black and white truffle in Oregon and then on Vancouver Island. Playing with the idea of hosting a wild mushroom and game promotion, I contacted Kathy Patterson, the woman who had discovered the truffle. She and her husband were truffle brokers. Kathy agreed to come to Toronto to help promote my idea.

Truffles grow underground but their strong aroma gives them away. In the old days, farmers used pigs on a leash to find them—and so, I decided, would we, with a little help from my friend Robin Leach.

Leslie Tell, co owner of the Bowmanville Zoo, said she could train her Vietnamese potbellied pig Betsy to search for truffles. In fact, the pig could do it at a press conference.

Truffle day arrived at the Old Mill. On cue, the gates flew open and two police officers on motorcycles roared in, sirens blaring, lights flashing. Then a white 1936 Rolls-Royce Phantom III limousine majestically entered. Out stepped Robin Leach with his signature glass of champagne in hand. I moved forward to greet him and introduced Kathy Patterson. Then Betsy arrived decked out in Tiffany diamonds. The reporters and photographers gathered for the ceremony howled with laughter.

Betsy proceeded to do her duty. She sniffed at the trail left by a liter of truffle oil and then trooped along, came to a stop, and began to paw the ground.

Good old Betsy found the truffles! Cue deafening applause.

The Old Mill's charm and warmth filled me with awe. It was easy to see the potential for it to grow into something truly magnificent. The Kalmars and I brainstormed all sorts of ideas: how the inn would eventually look inside and out, the services it could provide. We went to the surrounding community, presenting future projections, creating models, and even producing a video outlining our plans. Finally, we received approval for construction of a 60-room hotel.

But then George and Michael got cold feet. In order to be successful an average room rate of more than $200 would have to be charged, a lot of money back then. They hesitated. A renovated and expanded Old Mill did not finally open until October 2001. By that time I was long gone.

Chapter Twenty-eight

The next chapter of my life is filled with disappointment, personal and professional pain, embarrassment, and later, tragedy. It was not an easy time, and it made me begin to ask the questions that led to the writing of this book.

The pivotal character during this tumultuous period was a charismatic ex-priest named Ron Kelly, founder and chief executive officer of RHK Capital Inc. As a priest, he had for years served Cardinal Gerald Emmett Carter in the Toronto Archdiocese, overseeing Catholic cemeteries and the church's vast real estate holdings.

I met Ron in 1979 when he arranged the first annual dinner for Cardinal Carter at the Sheraton Centre. In 1984, I worked with him on Pope John Paul II's Canadian visit, acting as chairman of the pope's only formal dinner at the newly opened Metro Toronto Convention Centre.

A special office for the pope was set up, decorated with Persian carpets, $250,000 worth of antique furniture, and a direct telephone line to the Vatican. The Eaton family donated a "holy throne" in case his holiness required a bathroom. Arriving at the Metro Convention Centre, the pope glanced at his specially-built office, blessed it, and then moved on. That was as close as he ever got to it.

However, he did try to use the bathroom. As the pope waited, an RCMP officer tried to open the door.

Locked!

Everyone shuffled in embarrassment. The pope indicated he could wait and moved on. After everyone cleared the area, a red-faced young priest stumbled out of the bathroom. The pope never used it, either.

Dealing with Father Kelly in those days was a pleasure. He was always cheerful, intelligent, and courteous.

Once Ron left the church, he bought the abandoned Triumph Hotel in Toronto, reopened it, and made it a success. He had also bought the Toronto Airport Marriott Hotel and several apartment buildings that he then flipped for a substantial profit. He established himself among investors and banks as someone who possessed a magic touch, especially when it came to distressed properties.

After I left the Sutton Place, I occasionally ran into him, and we always talked about some day working together. Realizing that the Old Mill expansion plans were not going to happen any time soon, I again began to question myself and wonder about my future.

A friend, Stephen Phillips, president and CEO of Howard Johnson Hotels and Resorts, suggested I get in touch with Ron, who was talking about expanding his hotel division.

I met with him in his downtown office, and he shared his vision for RHK. He needed someone like myself who could help assess hotel operations in duress, why they were in the mess they were in, and what could be done to improve things for the least amount of money.

This was right up my alley. I had spent much of my career in marketing and promotions, assessing needs and building action steps to fulfill those needs. We talked for hours, and at the end of it Ron offered me a job—president and chief operating officer of RHK's hotel division.

At that point, RHK had one hotel in Toronto, the Triumph, another in Ottawa, the Chimo, and the Delta in St. John's, Newfoundland. The company had just acquired the Radisson in London, Ontario, re-flagging as a Westin Hotel.

My first mission in my new job was to scout the PineStone Inn, a 120-room resort and golf course, two and a half hours north of Toronto amid the rolling hills of Haliburton. It twice had gone into receivership, and it showed. However, the resort had a friendly group of employees, and the overall setting certainly showed potential. Less than a month after I saw it, the PineStone Inn became another RHK hotel.

Meanwhile, Ron was spending more time in the Bahamas, convinced the newly elected government of Prime Minister Hubert Ingraham would promote investment and development, as well as a friendlier environment for tourists.

For the first time in my professional life, I was doing a lot of business traveling, commuting almost weekly between the Bahamas and Jamaica in addition to frequent trips to the U.S. Not all the flying was pleasant. Somehow, I ended up in a red twin-engine Comanche plane, partially owned by Ron, en route to a New Brunswick meeting in the dead of winter.

Before boarding, I learned there was no life insurance for passengers. That should have been warning enough. The "new" life vests on board were from Canadian Tire, really cheap. The pilot had a hand-held GPS device since the onboard system did not function. Unbelievably, considering I had a wife and two children at home, I didn't immediately jump off the plane—another one of the many instances when I should have had my head read.

We arrived in Miramichi, New Brunswick safely enough. But there was no sign of the contact who was supposed to meet us. For good reason, it turned out. We had landed at the wrong airport.

We flew on to Moncton where there was an airport that could handle international traffic. As we left, I saw how ice could form on the wings within seconds. A scary sight, I assure you.

The next challenge was to find the airport at Saint John. That was easier said than done. I began to suspect there was a problem when the co-pilot turned the hand-held GPS device upside down, and announced that Saint John had to be down there somewhere.

Eventually, the clouds opened up enough for us to spot a huge runway. Somehow, we'd found Saint John, although I'm still not sure how we did it. That was enough for me. I decided to take a commercial flight back to Toronto. Lucky for me I did.

Somewhere over the Atlantic Ocean, the pilot, facing heavy head winds, decided to switch fuel tanks. In doing that, he shut off *all* the tanks. Both engines stopped. Only the sound of the whistling wind could be heard. The plane dropped toward the black ocean, falling a couple of thousand feet before the pilot got it restarted.

Meanwhile, I sat in Air Canada's business class section sipping my second—or was it third?—glass of chardonnay.

That is not to say that flying for RHK was always so dangerous. To the contrary. Once the company took over a private jet rental business, it became extremely pleasant and much faster in and out of airports. We owned three Lear jets as well as a larger Hawker that seated six to 10 passengers, staffed by two fulltime pilots. With two hotels in Jamaica and two in Nassau, I was in perpetual motion, flying off to the Caribbean almost weekly. There was also a lot of Canadian travel—it was almost as far to fly to our St. John's Delta Hotel as it was to the Bahamas.

Working in the islands was a constant challenge. All the things you have heard about life on the islands moving at a slower pace are true. You really do have to shift down a gear. It didn't help that I was an outsider. Over the years many islanders had seen investors come and go, often leaving behind failed businesses and bankruptcy. So we were often regarded with suspicion. It took time, hard facts, and dollar-driven investments to change people's minds.

The more time I spent in the Caribbean, the more I concluded that many people on the islands had not only run away from their previous lives but, in some cases, the law. They wanted to start over and figured the Bahamas was the right place to do it. By the time I met them, they were beginning to figure out it wasn't the right place at all. Often they were disappointed and bored. They resided in paradise, but paradise wasn't all it was cracked up to be. They worked hard at playing, but playing didn't make them happy. Just the opposite. I listened to complaints about fortunes won and lost, cellars full of wine that could no longer be consumed, ex-wives to whom millions had to be paid, and then more millions to new spouses.

The lifestyles of the rich and famous—I saw the part that Robin Leach never showed on his TV series.

Not that I didn't encounter some memorable characters.

One of those characters was a German, Peter Kugler, the biggest developer on Paradise Island.

Peter built himself a beautiful penthouse atop a condominium at the edge of the Paradise Island Airport. Gambling that the airport eventually would close to accommodate encroaching multi-million dollar developments, he put up not only with the noise but with planes just clearing the top of his penthouse.

He complained repeatedly to airport management about these brushes with death but to no avail. One day he had enough. He got out a flare gun and shot at a passing plane. Then he hopped into his golf cart, drove over to the airport onto the runway. When the plane door opened, he jumped on board, went into the cockpit and punched out the captain.

Somehow, he got away with it, although I can't imagine how.

Ludwig Meister, having started a bakery chain in Germany, moved to the Bahamas. Fascinated by dolphins, his villa was filled with every shape and size of dolphin in silver, granite, crystal, and wood. He always dreamed of swimming with dolphins, so he hired a trainer, enclosed an area of the beach, and at the age of 50, made his dream a reality. To swim next to a dolphin holding its fins, is one of those thrills of a lifetime you hear about but seldom experience. Ludwig got to experience it every day—and turned it into a lucrative business.

One of Ron Kelly's friends was an 80-year-old con man named John Doyle, an American who managed to convince Joey Smallwood's Liberal Newfoundland government to invest $142 million in his company, Javelin, promising to build paper and lumber mills and open mines to aid the province's chronic unemployment. None of it ever happened. Doyle, faced with 400 charges of fraud, escaped to Panama. By the time I met him, he was a lonely old man living in a vast penthouse. He had remarried but his wife was back in Miami, and he seldom saw her.

Over a couple of meals together, I thought I could detect the spark that allowed Doyle to fire the hopes of so many Newfoundlanders. He was so charming, the story goes, that he managed to sell Javelin shares to the two FBI agents investigating him. All these years later, Doyle was still defending himself, claiming the charges resulted from opposing political forces in Newfoundland. He was an innocent man.

For some reason, Ron liked Doyle and was impressed by him. In fairness, Doyle had valuable contacts and a knowledge of Panama politics that Ron could draw upon.

The 200-acre South Ocean Golf & Beach Resort in Nassau, Bahamas is located on the southwest end of the island, next to that fabled haunt of the very rich, Lyford Cay Club. Unlike Lyford Cay, however, South Ocean Golf & Beach had stumbled badly. Still, there was potential. It featured a mile-long swath of beach, a PGA-class golf course, an internationally known diving area at Stuart Cove (featured in several James Bond movies). It also had first dibs on the island's last gambling license.

The possibility of that license was all Ron needed. He bought the hotel at an auction but didn't tell me about it until after the Christmas holidays. No due diligence had been done; not that it would have mattered. The hotel's many deficiencies were obvious.

Ron's strategy was simple: spruce up the property and then find potential partners who could trigger further development.

South Ocean Golf & Beach Resort,
Bahamas, in dire need of restoration.

The problems started when it was proposed we spend a million dollars on landscaping. I argued that it was crazy to waste this kind of money when the basic operation needed work. Guests complained about everything, right down to the lack of knives and forks. Landscaping was the least of our problems. No one was going to look over the balcony and protest that a tree was missing. But everybody would complain about the lack of proper air-conditioning.

Eltha Deleveaux, our Bahamian general manager, and I, did our best to operate the property despite its shortcomings, but it was difficult to get anything done. For example, a public road ran right through the resort separating the hotel from villas on the beach. Cars often raced along the road at breakneck speed. Eventually, the government installed a traffic light, but that didn't stop the speeding. We applied to add speed bumps, but the application was repeatedly denied.

Finally, one day while having asphalt work done, we had the idea of building our own speed bumps. After that, cars slowed down—that is until the government sent out trucks to remove the speed bumps we had just installed. Nothing ever works fast in the islands—except where those speed bumps were concerned. The government had them out of there in a day.

Incidentally, the improvements to the hotel never did get made, and Ron never did get that gambling license.

Chapter Twenty-nine

A corporate battle had broken out between Rand V. Araskog, CEO of ITT, the conglomerate that owned the Sheraton Hotel chain, and Stephen Bollenbach, Hilton's CEO. The conflict started when Bollenbach launched a hostile takeover bid for ITT's Sheraton Hotels, publicly criticizing Araskog for not generating enough shareholder profit—not exactly an uncommon complaint in business. The fight between the two executives had become nasty and personal. Rand Araskog did not want to sell Sheraton to Hilton no matter how tantalizing the offer.

In the midst of this corporate wrangling, Ron and I arrived in New York for a meeting with Alan Kanders of Lehman Brothers. We were on a scouting mission to see if Lehman was interested either in lending us money or partnering in future investments. The meeting turned out to be of no real consequence. Following lunch atop the World Trade Center, Ron and I drove out to LaGuardia airport for the return to Toronto.

We talked about the Hilton-ITT battle. I thought there might be an opportunity to buy the crown jewel assets of Sheraton, thereby pre-empting Hilton's unfriendly strike. I asked Ron if he could raise a billion dollars. He said yes, for the right deal.

This, I suggested, might be that right deal.

In the limo on the way to the airport, we called Lehman and floated the idea. Come back, they said. We turned around and drove back to their Manhattan offices where I outlined my plan for acquiring Sheraton. Lehman Brothers said they wanted to be in on the deal.

My old contacts at Sheraton still worked. I called Stephen Foster, a senior vice president with the company in Toronto, and he passed me on to Sheila Schofield, the vice president of communications at Sheraton's head office in Boston. Within minutes I had a call from Rand Araskog's New York office. An appointment was set up for the following morning.

When Ron and I arrived, we met with Rand Araskog's executive assistant, Mark Thomas. Ron gave him a brief rundown as to who we were and my background working for Sheraton Hotels for 11 years. We had just met Lehman Brothers executives, he said, and they were willing to back our offer for Sheraton's St. Regis Hotel in New York as well as the St. Regis brand name. The offer included the Washington, D.C. Carlton Hotel and the Scottsdale Phoenician. Separately, we also wanted to make an bid for the Sheraton stake in the Italian CIGA Hotels.

We discussed a long-term deal with ITT Sheraton that would allow us to own these properties while Sheraton continued to manage them. However, if ITT Sheraton was ever taken over, the deal would be void. That's exactly what ITT wanted—generate cash for shareholders while hanging on to the management of the hotels. We agreed to come back in 10 days with a more formal proposal. In the meantime, we would send detailed background information on RHK Capital Inc.

Leaving their offices, I shook with excitement. This was an audacious play to be sure, a historic deal if we could pull it off. When we outlined the proposal to our lenders they—cautiously— agreed to take part. Ron began to see himself as an internationally recognized hotel tycoon.

For me, it would be the pinnacle of all my long-held career aspirations—much bigger than anything I might have dreamt in my wildest imaginings. I don't know how often I silently said "wow" to myself.

I did hear one note of caution.

When I called Helga from New York, she shared my excitement. However, she knew me better than anyone, knew that my reach could sometimes exceed my grasp. Be careful, she cautioned.

Fateful words, as it turned out.

On a Sunday in July 1997, Helga's birthday, my whole world fell apart.

I knew it was coming. But I wasn't prepared for how ruinous it would be. I don't think any of us were, although I'd had an inkling of trouble a few days before when Ron came into my office.

As soon as he entered, I could see the intense stress in his face. His voice was reduced to a hoarse whisper. The *Toronto Sun* was about to do a story about him. Certain allegations had been made years ago, and he was worried about what those allegations would do to his reputation and the reputation of the company if they should surface again.

Was there anything I could do to help?

I didn't fully understand what the allegations entailed and didn't press for details. Instead, I called my friend Paul Godfrey, who had become the *Sun* publisher. I wanted to know whether Ron should agree to talk to a *Sun* reporter. Paul made it clear that he would not and could not stop the article. He strongly suggested Ron tell his story so the paper wouldn't have to tell it for him.

Still not fully grasping what was about to unfold, I reported back to Ron. The next day we hired Tom MacMillan, a former *Sun* executive, now a specialist in executive crisis management control. Ron wouldn't talk about his past in front of me. I had to leave the office. I should have known.

That night I couldn't sleep. At five thirty the next morning I went down to the lobby of our apartment building. The *Sunday Sun* was lying on the floor. Ron was on the front page under a headline that read "From Priest to Tycoon."

I took the paper and went out and sat in the garden. I read the story,

And I cried.

In 1979, Ron Kelly was a young priest in the small Newfoundland town of Piccadilly. Accused of sexually abusing five boys between the ages of 13 and 17, he was arrested and convicted. Ron received a two-year suspended sentence. The prosecution appealed the lenient sentence, but it was upheld. A few months later, he was allowed to resume his duties and worked as a priest in two Ontario parishes before being transferred to the Archdiocese of Toronto to assist Cardinal Carter.

He oversaw church construction and in 1984 helped organize the Canadian visit of Pope John Paul II. The following year he received a pardon from the Conservative government of Prime Minister Brian Mulroney.

Shortly after that, Ron's name came up during the Hughes Inquiry looking into the abuse of boys at the notorious Mount Cashel orphanage. He protested that he had nothing to do with the infamous St. John's orphanage, but the revelation of his previous pedophile conviction resulted in him renouncing his vows and leaving the priesthood.

Now the *Toronto Sun* newspaper had once again resurrected the story. Ron's crimes had taken place over 20 years before, and he was said to have repented. But I couldn't help thinking about the young men whose lives he must have affected. How did he make it all the way into the cardinal's office? How could my former employers at the Sutton Place wine and dine him, as did so many others from bankers to politicians to business giants?

He had raised money for Prime Minister Jean Chrétien. Some of the most powerful people in Canada walked in and out our offices. Maybe they had forgiven him. After all, Ron had paid for his sins. Even Prime Minister Mulroney pardoned him. As a result, he had no criminal record. The article was old news. Wasn't it? Maybe someone wanted revenge. But why? Why now? We were just days away from a history-making business deal, and now all of that was in grave jeopardy.

When I finally went back upstairs and showed the story to Helga and my sons, they were as upset as I was. We sat and talked together about what I should do next. My dealings with him over the years had all been above board, despite our disagreements. Now he needed my support. In the article, he blamed what happened on his alcoholism. But he had not touched a drop in years. George Mallon, Sheraton's comptroller, knew him as a priest and had the highest regard for Father Ron. So many people with so many good words to say about him. Were they all wrong, including me?

After hours of discussion with my family, I leaned toward believing that whatever had happened, happened a long time ago. Ron had changed. I decided to go to work the next day.

Ron arrived early as well, and we had a coffee together. In his whispery voice he told me how much the article hurt him, the emotions it had once again stirred up. His two brothers, Hubert and John, supported him over the weekend. Ron told me how much they suffered. The one thing I noticed amid all Ron's reports of weekend suffering, he said nothing about the suffering of his victims.

I asked Ron to address the staff. He said he was too upset. Could I do it? Reluctantly, I agreed. However, I thought it was something he should have done. I sensed the sadness of everyone in the office as I repeated what I had already worked out in my mind—as upsetting as the article was, Ron had paid his debt to society. He had tried to make amends for his crimes, and he had been a good boss to us all. We had to stick together and support him.

Did I really believe what I told the staff? I'm not sure I did. But I said those things that Monday at the office, and I suppose it worked because nobody quit.

Ron and I returned to New York the night before the ITT Sheraton meeting, armed with support letters from Cardinal Carter, business leaders, bank presidents, politicians, friends, and family. We might as well have saved the paper. At dinner I told the

Lehman rep about the *Sun* story. He paled noticeably, and then stood up and announced he was out of the deal. As far as he was concerned, Lehman Brothers was out as well.

He also strongly suggested that we call Rand Araskog's office before going over there. The next morning, I made the call from Ron's suite at the St. Regis and told Araskog's assistant about the newspaper article. "Don't waste our time," came the curt reply a moment before the phone slammed down.

Even without hearing my phone conversation, Ron knew the meeting was off and so was the deal. We climbed on an early plane back to Toronto. Neither of us said much. Dreams had been shattered that morning. Again, I questioned myself: should I quit?

I've spent a great deal of time over the years reviewing the details of what went wrong. I believe it had as much to do with the heated corporate battle being waged between Sheraton and Hilton as it did with Ron's past. Any whiff of scandal would have brought the sort of attention Sheraton simply was not prepared to deal with. At another time in another place, all might have been forgiven. But at that time in that place, no one was willing to give us the benefit of the doubt.

Chapter Thirty

After he had time to digest the Sheraton failure, Ron became more determined than ever. "If the press thinks I'm a tycoon," he said, referring to the *Toronto Sun* headline, "then I will be one." The reinvigorated tycoon bought a Bentley, then traded it in for a $300,000 Rolls-Royce. He bought more jets and used them often.

Besides his estate in Newmarket, the former home of Magna's Frank Stronach, Ron purchased a second house in Nassau. He acquired a chalet at Mont Tremblant, Quebec, as well as an apartment in Montreal. There was a large estate in Newfoundland, a penthouse in Panama, and a townhouse on Lake Simcoe, north of Toronto.

We moved to a prestigious corner building at the corner of Wellington and Yonge Street in downtown Toronto. Ron was an admirer of newspaper mogul Conrad Black. The new office building reminded me of Black's Toronto Street address. Conrad also had a Rolls Royce.

By now Ron was on a tear, buying a hotel in Kingston, Jamaica and a smaller property in Ochos Rios. We were flying everywhere—Winnipeg, Montreal, Mont Tremblant, the islands of St. Kitts,

Nassau's British Colonial Hilton
following restoration.

Turks and Caicos, Jamaica, Belize, Haiti. Much of our time was spent being fêted by prime ministers and government officials anxious for investment dollars.

One of the hotels RHK bought during that period was Nassau's historic British Colonial Hotel. Originally built by the famous railway tycoon and entrepreneur Henry Flagler, many islanders had a personal history with the Colonial. Grandparents, parents, aunts and uncles, worked there at one time or another, and it was famous around the world thanks to its former owner, Sir Harry Oakes.

Oakes was an American geologist who, after panning for gold in Australia and California, finally found it in Kirkland Lake, Ontario. By the time he arrived in Nassau in 1935 and checked into the British Colonial, he had become a very rich man.

The hotel, oblivious to his wealth, in part because Harry was not the world's best dresser, treated him badly. Harry reacted by buying the hotel on the spot and immediately firing every employee who had been disrespectful. Despite that initial introduction, Harry stayed in the Bahamas, became a British citizen, a member of parliament,

British Colonial Hilton gala opening celebration.

and a powerful developer who was eventually knighted.

In 1943, Sir Harry was found beaten to death, his body partially burned. No one was ever convicted of his murder, although various books and movies have proposed a number of suspects, the most popular being Sir Harry's son-in-law, Count Alfred de Marigny, even though he was tried for the crime and found not guilty.

So now we had a famous hotel once owned by an infamous island resident. The question was, what to do with it? We decided on a $100 million renovation, stripping the old place down to its bare bones and then rebuilding. Ron promised the prime minister, the historical society, and the people of the Bahamas, that he would keep the hotel's historical identity intact. He did just that at great expense. I give him full credit.

Nonetheless, a fight soon developed over the second-floor ballroom and convention center. Hilton's corporate food and beverage director convinced Ron that there should be a signature restaurant and bar on that floor.

I argued that besides the additional cost of building and operating a separate kitchen, the restaurant would compromise the privacy of the convention center. Worse, the restaurant would be away from the general traffic and thus unable to attract walk-in business.

I pushed for a steak and seafood restaurant in the main lobby. I lost the argument. They went ahead and built the Wedgwood, a fine dining room and bar on the second floor with a separate kitchen tucked away in a corner. It never worked. Less than a year later, it was abandoned at a cost of millions.

For the official ceremony marking the reopening of what was now called the British Colonial Hilton, we invited guests from all over the world. Even Ron Kelly's friend, Cardinal Emmett Carter, showed up. Eight hundred people, including Bahamian Prime Minister Hubert Ingraham, gathered at the foot of the dramatic staircase that was the hotel entrance. Ron took the microphone and thanked everyone who had ever lifted a hammer in the building.

Everyone that is, except me.

On that magical opening night, there were no apologies for the oversight and no explanations. Helga never forgave him for the cheap shot.

Then in the late summer of 2000, I was diagnosed with prostate cancer.

In denial, not wanting to face up to my condition, to my family's dismay I postponed treatment for six months. A good friend called from New York's Sloan-Kettering Cancer Institute one day after his prostate operation, urging me to do what had to be done. That finally woke me up. I made the appointment and was scheduled for surgery at the end of April 2001.

In the meantime, RHK's investors had grown increasingly nervous. The cash-flow projections were too optimistic given the slow revenue, renovation delays, cost overruns, and major currency exchange fluctuations we were experiencing. There was a growing suspicion Ron was spreading himself too thin and not staying focused. The dialogue between the lenders and Ron became more strained. Besides clipping his wings in terms of corporate expenses, steps were taken to shed some of the investments he made.

Perhaps I was too sympathetic to our investors, or maybe he sensed my continuing uneasiness about his past. Whatever the reason, relations between myself and Ron had cooled dramatically. My responsibilities were sharply reduced. I had been running the South Ocean Resort and had been more or less living there. But in the fall of 2000 I was moved back to Toronto and told to keep an eye on our Canadian properties. By now there were not a lot of Canadian properties to keep an eye on. The Delta St. John's had been sold, Ottawa's Chimo Hotel and the Triumph Hotel in Toronto were both on the auction block. That left only the Delta PineStone in Haliburton.

In March 2001, Ron called everyone together and announced that the company had gone under. Difficult economic times had caught up with us, he said. Lenders were taking over the assets. The Caribbean properties were to be managed by a local team based in Nassau. He gave us all two weeks notice. We could leave sooner if we wanted.

In the end, RHK was a victim of the bad economic environment. The lenders had become nervous looking at business-revenue projections originally based on a booming economy; at the end of the millennium, the times had ceased to boom. What's more, the company borrowed Canadian funds which then had to be converted into U.S. dollars during a time when the value of the loonie fell to 67 cents against the U.S. dollar. That meant that if we needed $10 million in U.S. funds we actually had to borrow $13 million. It was all simply too much.

Chapter Thirty-one

I started this story on a horrific day in September 2001, a day that left me questioning the validity of life. Why? I asked myself constantly during those bleak, dark days following the World Trade Center collapse and Ralph's death. *Why? Why? Why?* I remembered moments seared in memory from those terrible days: giving a DNA sample, signing Ralph's death certificate, standing in Ralph's empty apartment after the movers left, having one more look around, recalling how happy he was here.

Moments keep coming back. Moments I'll never forget.

As I come to the end of the story so far, I must admit I'm not so sure I have any answers to the questions I've been asking myself for the past 10 years. I get as close as you probably can by realizing how lucky I have been, all in all. How lucky I was to find Helga and to have two great children. How fortunate I was to come to Canada after a world war and miserable deprivation and to have an opportunity to work in the industry I love so much, to meet all the wonderful and talented people who have passed through my life. Fortunate, too, that I am usually forgiven my many shortcomings.

I keep remembering the time I gave my sons hell for not

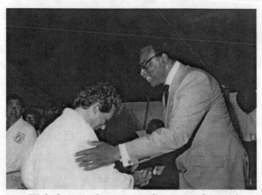

*With Ontario Lieutenant Governor General
Lincoln Alexander after a lake relay swim.*

arranging anything to celebrate Mother's Day. That was because
Stephan and Ralph had arranged and paid for something else: a
surprise 25th anniversary black-tie dinner for Helga and myself.
They invited 25 couples, including my sister Gitta, and brother-
in-law Rudolf, their son Thomas, and daughter Tina. That night
Helga and I renewed our vows. Reason enough right there to go
on living.

I've been given so much, all in all, and therefore have tried
to give something back. Over the years I involved myself in as
many local and national charities as I could fit in. I swam Lake
Ontario, drove 100 miles across a frozen lake on a snow machine,
raced in a hot air balloon, competed in bed-making contests, sold
bricks donated from the pub set of British TV's long-running
Coronation Street, played in innumerable charity golf and tennis
tournaments, and generally tried to help people who could not
help themselves.

There has been triumph in my life and, God knows, tragedy.
My brother Guenther, after a difficult life, was killed riding his
bike, hit by a drunken neighbor woman's car at six in the morning,
then dragged along the street and decapitated. The driver fled the
scene. The tremendous pain and shock of his death hung over our
family, particularly Guenther's wife Erna, his son Klaus Dieter, and
daughter Sabine.

Ralph with his girlfriend Linda Luzzicone, who also died at the World Trade Center.

And as I rewrite these final pages, Helga and I just returned from Washington, D.C. where we buried beautiful 18-year-old Jordan, the daughter of Christine, my son Stephan's wife. Yet another great shock and a huge loss to our family.

Life can be so cruel, but then you discover how many friends and even strangers have generously shared in your grief and tried to comfort you. You reflect on the time you had with your loved ones, wishing you had more time with them, and then you laugh, remembering so many happy moments.

The beauty of those you love and what they really meant often comes out only when they are gone. Our son Ralph had a special gift. "He lived to live," his brother Stephan says.

Ralph had the power of now. When you talked to him, he

was only listening to you. He made you feel that your words were most important to him. Few people have that gift. I try to remind myself to do the same; *listen*. Words mean something. When time has passed, you cannot rewind the clock. You must treasure every moment and use the words "not now" less.

Ralph worked for Howard Lutnick, the chief executive officer of Cantor Fitzgerald. In addition to Ralph and Linda, the firm lost 658 employees that September day, the company's entire headquarters office. Howard also lost his brother Gary and his best friend, Doug Gardener. He told me later that it was his son's first day at school, otherwise, he would have been inside the building when the plane struck.

In the first moments after the tragedy, Howard did some things and made public statements that, rather than helping families get through the tragedy, infuriated many of us. But then we were angry at the world in general for taking away our loved ones.

Howard, to his credit, listened to that anger and changed his approach. Today, I can't say enough about him and his sister Edie, and what the company has done for all of us. Cantor's generosity and assistance, particularly for families with children, went far beyond what other companies affected by 9/11 have done.

New York was always special to us but even more so now because that's where Ralph is. We returned to the city in late October 2001 for a memorial and again on December 1 when Mayor Rudy Giuliani declared Canada Day in the city. This time we did not come alone. Twenty thousand Canadians joined in the salute to New Yorkers as part of a "Canada Loves New York" campaign. The event was created by Canadian Senator Jerry Grafstein and his wife Carol, along with George Cohon and many others, including myself.

Well-known Canadian artist Charles Pachter created *Side by Side*, a painting of the Canadian and American flags designed not only to celebrate Ralph but to remind Americans of Canadians' wholehearted support. He later donated another painting of the flags in Ralph's memory to the U.S. Consulate in Toronto.

We were in New York on New Years Eve 2001, stuck in the Holland Tunnel during a bomb scare. Horrifying moments, yet another reminder that the terrorism threat that killed Ralph and so many others was never far away.

The next day I hosted a "Salute to Vienna" New Year's Day concert at Lincoln Center and had a chance to thank New Yorkers for the wonderful support they showed us and all 9/11 families.

A Cantor Fitzgerald tribute in Central Park to those who died touched me deeply. Our friends Patti and Robert Pilon accompanied us to the memorial. Robert sang. I spoke, thanking Howard, Edie, the Cantor Team, and the citizens of New York.

I concluded by saying, "To the world, Ralph Gerhardt was one of the World Trade Center victims. To us, Ralph *was* the world."

Senator Hillary Clinton followed me on stage. As we passed, she touched my arm and murmured, "That was very powerful."

The touch of an understanding hand. The murmur of sympathy from a stranger. Memories. Why we live—and keep on.

Side by Side *painting by Charles Pachter.*

Epilogue

Egyptian hotelier Ibrahim Fahmy says it's the bed. As far as he is concerned, the hotel room bed, the way it is constructed, the quality of the linens and pillows, has vastly improved over the past 10 years and that is one of the biggest changes he has seen in the business. Interesting perspective.

Others believe technology has revolutionized the business. I tend to agree, although there are any number of forces at work, including lifestyle and economics, as well as new marketing and merchandising techniques.

Whatever has changed, you can bet its been done on a computer—everything is computerized now. Ian Barbour, an asset manager and consultant for a major Four Seasons hotel investor, urges the embrace of technology but not at the expense of compromising guest services. Good advice, and the best hotels tend to follow it. Still, it's hard to personalize service when so much of it is outsourced.

Gone are the butchers, bakers, patissiers, launderers, and security that traditionally were part of a hotel's staff. Outside companies now provide those services. They also take care of hotel restaurants, parking, even maid and concierge services.

Old-fashioned hospitality: greeting the Queen Mother.

The question constantly asked is this: is today's customer better served by all these changes? The answer is, yes, most likely. But at the same time, the soul of the business has somehow been lost. Ibrahim Fahmy, area vice president of Starwood Egypt, put it this way: "The Grand Hotel is still there but the grandeur is gone."

Family-owned hotels passed from generation to generation hardly exist anymore. Large chains have brought a uniformity which is good for customers in the sense they know what to expect. But perhaps that's part of the problem, too: they know what to expect.

Still, if something does go wrong, there is a large chain that can muster resources to take care of the problem. In this age of terrorism and epidemics such as SARS and the Swine Flu, those fears have re-shaped the behavior of hotel chains. Major lawsuits have also created a much greater awareness of the innkeepers' responsibilities.

Diving boards used to be a standard feature of hotel pools. Lawsuits did away with them. Some changes are for the better.

When singer Connie Francis was raped at the Howard Johnson Mayfair Hotel in New York, she sued. As a result, peep holes are now standard in hotel rooms.

The late Professor Tony Marshall of Florida State University, one of the best motivational speakers, stressed the practice of "reasonable care" to prevent lawsuits. If, for example, there is a tear in the carpet or a spill on the floor and it cannot be attended to immediately, at least put up a sign to warn guests. More good advice.

Hotel chains now insist on conformity, and owners must comply with corporate standards and put an allowance aside for renovations. Four Seasons Hotels and Resorts, for example, insists on a three to four percent reserve of funds taken from the top of total revenue for FF & E (Furniture, Fixtures and Equipment) in order to maintain their standards.

I met with Michael Beckley, senior vice president of Marriott Development, just after he came off one of those no-service airplane flights—not the best time to discuss anything. He lamented that the fun has gone out of traveling, the adventure was missing from a hotel stay. The short term financial goals of investors versus the long-term objectives of hoteliers are vastly different in today's business world.

Industry cycles of three years down and seven years up often get caught between the hotel industry's professional standards versus investors' demand for profits. Short-term goals compromise the soul of hotels. Non-revenue-producing areas such as pools and fitness clubs are still must-haves for a good hotel, but in the old days so were dining rooms, bars, and clubs—they created the heart of a hotel, not to mention a good deal of its traffic. In today's business model, they are either eliminated, downsized, or outsourced.

Internet wholesalers demand the lowest rates with no concern for the quality of service. While independent and boutique hotels still try to provide personalized hospitality, name brand hotel chains seem interested only in generating maximum profits, no matter what.

William Meloche, frequent traveler and communications specialist for the Meloche Group, yearns for the bygone time of gracious hospitality when there were fine dining rooms, a real bar, and staff recognized returning guests by name and knew their preferences.

"The hotel's staff was a welcome respite from the calamitous business day I had just experienced," he says. "Today, hotel chains present a sameness that is flat-out boring and lonely. They are a place to sleep. End of story."

Angus Wilkinson, the president and CEO of Tyne Hospitality Services, misses the pride and passion of the old days. Over the past 50 years, he argues, the hotel industry has evolved into an impersonal profit-generating business.

The good news is that there is no shortage of talented people fighting to maintain traditional standards of quality and excellence.

Randy Morton, the president and CEO of the Bellagio Resort Casino Corporation, talks about the importance of creating a more powerfully unique experience for every guest. To help make that happen, the relationship between management and employees becomes all-important.

The Four Seasons Hotels became the global leader in the mid-1970s, says Antoine Corinthios, president of the company's Europe-Middle East-Africa division, by making the guest experience beyond comparison. He says the experience in a hotel must be positive and engaging, catering to the personal needs of the guests.

Horst Schulze, former president and chief operating officer of Ritz Carlton, agrees. He now runs his own company, West Paces Hotel Group, and he dedicates himself to continually trying to improve the guest experience. Today's traveler is much more sophisticated, he says. New concepts must be constantly developed to keep up with that sophistication.

John Williams, executive vice president of Fairmont Raffles Hotels and Resorts, says it is difficult to predict the future of hotels given the rapid changes during the last decade. However, the next generation certainly will research their hotel before they leave home, and will benefit tremendously from first-class brand associations.

Online promises of service and product will be challenged by the sophisticated customer who insists on exemplary service. There will be greater demand for high-tech hotel rooms, luxury bathrooms, and eco-friendly properties. Why should guests stay in surroundings inferior to their own homes?

As it was a half a century ago, excellence of service will be the defining difference in hotels, and the service winners will continue to thrive and provide the greatest returns to investors and customers.

Or maybe at the end of the day, no matter what kind of change roils the industry, it all comes down to what Conrad Hilton advised when, in another age, he appeared on Johnny Carson's *Tonight Show*.

"Please put the shower curtain *inside* the tub."

Acknowledgements

I've written of the events in this book to the best of my recollection, prompted by the journals I kept for almost 40 years. I've checked certain facts and incidents with family, friends, and colleagues. To find out about my father, I attended seminars in Dresden, Germany, Washington, D.C., and in Huntsville, Alabama.

In 1996, I found documents outlining my father's battle with the West German authorities over the pension he was denied because the government claimed he voluntarily went to Russia after the war. Of course that could not be further from the truth.

My son Stephan was also a great help in uncovering my father's story. He introduced me to the Smithsonian Aerospace Museum's curator, professor Michael Neufeld, who referred me to Professor Olaf Przybilski of the Technical University in Dresden. Professor Przybilski's knowledge of Peenemünde and the German achievements after the war, particularly in Russia, was most enlightening.

Eventually, I met Christa Schwarz who lived as a child in Khimki, Russia, where her father, Willi, worked with my father. She showed me photographs that led to my discovery of a half brother from my father's relationship with Ilse Neumeister, the woman who was, in effect, Mrs. Gerhardt during my father's time in Russia.

I still keep in contact with Werner Baum, who led the team at Khimki. He has shared many details of life in Peenemünde and at Khimki. In his 90s, he is one of the few rocket specialists still alive.

There is so much in this life I could never have done without the help and support of my wife Helga and son Stephan. This book is no exception. In reconstructing a life, we shared many happy and sad memories. I am grateful and a lucky man to have Helga and Stephan at my side.

The Four Gs.

Danke Schoen.
I also would like to remember my late sister Gitta who lost

her courageous battle with cancer in August 2010. If she hadn't arrived in Canada, loved it, and urged me to follow, who knows what might have happened to me.

Many people played a part in changing my life and shaping me into who I am today. Eugen Christen in Itzehoe was one of these people. George Schwab, Frans Schutzman, and Kai Herbranson were the greatest hoteliers I ever met. They taught me more than they will ever know.

Reg Bovaird, my "fan" and friend. When Reg died Bill Burke Sr. said after his memorial that Reg was one of his closest friends. The best thing about Reg is that *everyone* thought he was their closest friend!

His dream was to celebrate his 65th birthday leading a parade of 250 friends that included the mayor of Toronto, the police chief, a judge, 12 Sunshine Girls, the Argo football team's cheerleaders, and the 55-piece Variety Village Band he founded. That's exactly what happened. His friend Ralph Sazio knocked on his door at 6 a.m. and delivered a specially printed edition of the *Toronto Sun*. Ralph also gave him a custom-tailored jacket a la *The Music Man* and a four-foot ceremonial baton. Reg almost fainted when he saw all his friends singing "Happy Birthday." He than proceeded to lead everyone around the block to where a tent had been erected. Orange juice and champagne was poured, flapjacks with maple syrup served, a dream made a reality.

Freddy Gallaugher, Reg's sidekick for years in the beer business, is another friend I always will remember. My pal Al Dubin who always began every argument over the cost for his special events with, "Hans, it's for the kids at Variety Village!"

Bill and Dorothy Burke, sons Bill Jr. and Michael, for printing thousands of *Healing Hearts* books in memory of our son Ralph. The book recounted stories of the dedicated emergency workers, firemen, and police who were the true heroes that day.

The great team of professionals I had the pleasure of working with for many years: Bernard Bictache, finance; executive chef Niels Kjeldsen and his sous chefs Brian Morin and John Higgins;

Ron Merpaw and Hans Stuerzenbecher in catering, Manuel Vaz in banquets; Dermot McKeown, Dale and Bernd Bohl, Ann Meadows my former assistants; concierges Lanfranco Gualandi and Peter Bone, the effervescent Len Kleine, a man of many talents. Klaus Tenter, my former competitor and friend, along with Josef Ebner and the gang at the Baker's Dozen, who funded the reception following the 9/11 memorial for Ralph. Ibrahim Fahmy, for hosting the New York reception for Ralph. Fred Pristine and his son Luan of Pristine Printing, for the 1,000 postcards with Ralph's picture. They also were kind enough to print the programs for the memorial service in honor of Ralph. Jim Magee, Ralph's former boss and his team at ShorCan, for their generosity and caring.

New York police officer John Trimmer, his wife, Sue, and sons, Matthew and Kevin. Officer Trimmer along with Bill Doyle kept the 9/11 families informed. And one more big thank you to the Cantor Fitzgerald team for all they have done: Howard and Edie Lutnick, Marianna Taaffe, Stuart Fraser, Jim Ficarro, Arlene, Sharon, and Juliet Rich. Also, Manfred Gau with whom I worked in Berlin in the mid-1960s. The events of 9/11 reunited us in 2006.

Loyal friends George and Susie Cohon; George was also a great customer who brought many McDonald events to the places I worked. We met at the Hyatt Regency Hotel in 1972, and have been in touch ever since. George has been always available when needed and even produced a video in memory of Ralph.

Ken McGowen, immediately on the phone, asking how he could help. Peter Kircher: "Are you okay and what can I do for you?" Kai Herbranson, who let me get away with many things at work, and David Hamilton who supported me in (most) cases.

What can I say about Catherine McAuley? We worked together for almost 20 years and she deserves so much credit for the fun and laughter, the joy, passion, and energy she brought to the table. And what a contribution she made to this book with her fact-checking. While she was working on the manuscript, a page blew into the lake. She jumped after it—fully clothed!

Gary Reinblatt, always ready to listen and provide advice.

*2008 Sheraton Hotel reunion
with Kai Herbranson.*

Harvey Hirsh, besides being my accountant, is a friend, and we shared many common interests from cars to business. My long-time friends on the Sheraton concourse level: David Punzo, Nat Mansour, Elaine and Mel Goodman. Also, Jim Clare, my co-conspirator planning so many special events.

George Christy, who introduced me to many of his friends and opened up the world of entertainment for me. Robin Leach, with whom I shared more than one bottle of Roederer Cuvée Cristal, and many laughs as we helped each other over the years.

Paul and Gina Godfrey, thank you for being friends. Gina involved me in her wonderful charity, the Herbie Fund. I loved working with her and the so-called Glitter Girls, (see Rosemary Sexton's book *The Glitter Girls*): Catherine Nugent, Carole Grafstein, Cathy Bratty, Pat Appleton, Anna Maria de Sousa, Marilyn Lastman, Nancy Paul, Bluma Appel, Barbara Kingstone, Daniella Bruns, Judi Cohen, Evelyn Huang.

Meeting my teenage idol, singer Freddy Quinn, and his musical director, Joe Kirsten: memories are made of this. Michael Sloan, my good friend and loyal customer. Director George Mendeluk, another loyal customer. Dusty Cohl, how I miss this guy.

Doug Creighton and his wife Marilyn and their three sons, Scott, Bruce, Donald and "adopted" son, Ron Mitchell. Former *Sun* sports editor, George Gross, remembered always for his friendship. Dr. Marty Taylor and wife Leila, our trusted doctor and friends. Trudy and Robert Bundy; Trudy being the ultimate effervescent optimist. Bob Antoniou, for friendship and generosity; Canada's number one hotel realtor, Bill Stone as well as Lyle Hall for their support.

Paul Graham, who battled Parkinson's for the past 21 years, is so fortunate to be surrounded by a loving family—wife Helen, daughters Andrea and Claire.

Melissa and David Freeborn-Merchant, Ralph's friends, who generously introduced Marc Gottridge, who in turn introduced us to Gottlieb Sterns lawyers Roland Chase and Nick Cottagio. They compassionately guided us through the legal quagmire following 9/11.

Ralph Lean for always having an open ear and a suggestion. John Bitove Sr. for offering help and advice. Marge and Allen Linden—Allen recently retired after 30 years as a Supreme Court judge—for sharing moments of joy and laughter. Robert Pilon and his beautiful wife Patti, who were always there for us.

Tim Lilleyman, who credits me with being his mentor but takes every opportunity to question it. Former Toronto mayor and now senator, Art Eggleton, for being a friend and making me "deputy mayor" while twinning the cities of Toronto and Frankfurt. Dan Almey who makes working together so much fun.

Peter Herrndorf and his wife Eva Czigler for their support and friendship. The always-entertaining Alan Eagleson, his wife Nancy and family. Charlie Lehoczky and Jill MacCurdy, including Ralph's godson Nicholas, brother Alex, and sister Katherine. Darcy and Brigitte Hall, daughters Madeleine and Allison. Mark and Fiona and daughter Amanda Schrader. Ralph's good friend and our little angel in New York, Robin McKenna. Sandra Porter and her partner Bob Murray for their moral support.

Monte Kwinter, for years of friendship and advice and also for standing up at Queens Park to ask for a moment of silence in memory of Ralph and all the 9/11 victims. Rudy Behring, who, with help from the citizens of St. Catharines, initiated the first memorial for Canadian 9/11 victims along the shores of Lake Ontario.

Over the years I worked with so many of the media, including my patient editor Ron Base, formerly of the *Toronto Star*, Sid Adilman, Rita Zekas, Rob Salem, Martin Knelman, Andy Donato, Liz Braun, Joan Sutton, Norm Betts, Lou Clancy, Mike Filey, Brett Halliday, Brian Linehan, George Anthony, Trisha Hickey, Barbara Kingstone, Rosemary Sexton, Zena Cherry, the Lombardi family at CHIN radio, Jill Rigby, Michael Hanlon, Jim Slotek, Mike Strobel, Marion Kane, Paul King, Glenn Cochrane, Carl Banas, Don Daynard, Jeremy Brown, Jerry Good, Bill Herz, Ron Hewat, Jim Paulson, Sandy Hoyt, James Chatto, Tony Aspeler, Jim Robinson, Jay Scott, Bruce Kirkland, Gary Dunford, Brenda Burns, Ken King, John Hinnen, Dini Petty, Ann Rohmer, Rosemary Goldhar, Party Barbara Hershenhorn, Brock Stewart, Diane Francis, Tom Sandler, Rosemary and Rolf Meyer, Erin Davis, Julie Stoddart, Bob Ramsay, Stephen LeDrew, Bill Baxter, Bill Anderson, Libby Znaimer, Rosanna Caira. I enjoyed working with all of them. I'd also like to thank producer Don Carmody, Dan Heffner, Chuck Fries, and Naish McHugh, former head of the Toronto Film Commission.

Lorraine Thompson and her husband, Knowlton Nash, for many years of cheerful friendship. The Mirvish family, for planting trees in Israel in Ralph's memory. Ken Shaw, Rick Henderson, and Jo Millage for arranging the Ralph Gerhardt Foundation Golf Tournament in Freeport, among many other good deeds. Mafalda Caruso of CTV for her help and for introducing me to David Pisarek, who created and hosted our son's website after 9/11 and who acted as our photographer at the Canada Loves New York campaign. Senator Jerry Grafstein who headed the committee that brought 20,000 Canadians to New York to celebrate Canada Loves New York on December 1, 2001—and Pamela Wallin, New York's Canadian Consul General during those awful days, for her kindness to the visiting victims' families.

I must also thank all the friends whether we knew them or not for their generous contributions to the Ralph Gerhardt Fund allowing hundreds of young, underprivileged children to attend summer camp. The fund also sponsors the annual Junior Achievement Ralph Gerhardt Company of the Year Award, as well as the annual Principal-Student Award at Ralph's former collegiate in Don Mills.

I started out writing 120,000 words to tell my story. We are now down to about 65,000 words because of the efforts of my editor, Ron Base, and copy editor Alexandra Lenhoff, both of whom worked long and patiently on the manuscript. Also, Julie Rekai Rickerd for her insights and advice at the beginning of the editing process and again at the end. A very special Danke Schoen.

A word of thanks to Jimmy Hattori and Carol Lau at Grenville Printing, for their hard work preparing the photos that illustrate this book. And to designer John Grant who brought so much talent to the cover design. More thanks go to Ric Base who designed the inside of the book and worked so hard laying out the photographs. And finally, to West-End Books publisher Brian Vallée for all his help in making this book a reality.

In taking out some great stories, I have probably lost names I should have mentioned. Please forgive me if I did, but you know who you are, and I appreciate you being part of my life.

Thank you all for being friends to Helga, Stephan, and me.

CPSIA information can be obtained at www.ICGtesting.com
Printed in the USA
LVOW12s0326191013

357612LV00001B/17/P

9 780973 695526